Leadership in Agriculture

Texas A&M AgriLife Research and Extension Service Series
Craig Nessler and Douglas L. Steele, General Editors

Leadership in AGRICULTURE

Case Studies for a New Generation

John Patrick Jordan, Gale A. Buchanan,
Neville P. Clarke & Kelly C. Jordan

Texas A&M University Press   •   College Station

This paper meets the requirements
of ANSI/NISO Z39.48-1992 (Permanence of Paper).
Binding materials have been chosen for durability.

General editors for this series are Craig Nessler, director of Texas A&M AgriLife
Research, and Douglas L. Steele, director of the Texas A&M AgriLife Extension
Service.

LIBRARY OF CONGRESS CATALOGING-IN-PUBLICATION DATA

Leadership in agriculture : case studies for a new generation /
John Patrick Jordan ... [et al.]. — 1st ed.
p. cm.—(AgriLife Research and Extension Service series)
Includes bibliographical references and index.
ISBN 978-1-60344-941-0 (cloth : alk. paper) —
ISBN 1-60344-941-8 (cloth : alk. paper) —
ISBN 978-1-60344-961-8 (e-book) —
ISBN 1-60344-961-2 (e-book)
1. Agricultural administration—United States—Case studies.
2. Leadership—United States—Case studies.   I. Jordan, John Patrick.
II. Series: AgriLife Research and Extension Service series.
S441.L33   2013
630.68—dc23
2012029624

Contents

Preface

Of all the requirements for maintaining life, the primary one for all living things is an adequate supply of food. Without it, starvation and death occur. The creation and growth of a food supply brought about by successful *agriculture* has remained fundamental throughout human history in spite of drought, floods, economic depressions, wars, and other challenges. Without leadership, these crises can indeed be overwhelming to humankind. Within less than a century, the agricultural system in developed countries—by employing sound science and technology and utilizing visionary leadership—has been able to yield a plentiful food supply for much of humanity and promises to do so for many years to come. Unfortunately, this is in contrast to the lack of adequate food in some parts of the world, which has been caused by poor political decisions or food-distribution mechanisms.

The focus of this book is the issue of leadership needed to ensure the continued adequate supply of food for humans, feed for livestock and companion animals, fiber for homes and clothes, and fuel and forestry necessary to meet human needs. The leadership issues discussed involve new solutions through research, production organizations, government efforts, universities as a knowledge base, and industrial distribution of food in a worldwide economy. The book identifies and proposes approaches for dealing with gaps in perspectives of leadership in the food and agriculture system. It focuses on the key characteristics and elements of leadership. It draws on case studies to illustrate the following:

How individual and group leadership produced outcomes of merit

How no one person is an island (i.e., is shared leadership a verti-
cal or a horizontal system of engagement of leaders or both?)
How leadership promotes/provokes new initiatives
How leadership gathers consensus and support
How leadership leads to an organizational commitment
How leadership develops a pathway to success
How leadership results in a sustained and sustainable result

Why Do We Need a Document about Leadership in Agriculture?

Many who are in agriculture are focusing on the technical aspects
of production, processing, financing, distribution, or the development of new knowledge. Often excellent people with technical skills
are asked to "move up" in the organization, first into middle-orga-
nization slots and perhaps later into upper-leadership positions. In
this publication, however, we address leadership as much more than
just management. Management is only one of the tools of leadership.
Management is a "how-to" effort, while leadership is a "focus" effort.
Although the definition of leadership is contained in this book, in
simple terms it is *motivating people to follow the leader in a specific
direction.* Leadership is manifest in conceptualizing, planning, and
implementing actions for a specific purpose.

We asked ourselves a set of questions and made observations on
how leadership emerges today:

What's good and bad about the way leadership emerges today?
Is it a wonder that it works at all?
Can the process of identifying and nurturing leadership be made
more efficient?
Can leaders be identified earlier in their careers and guidance
provided to make them more productive sooner?

Exactly what do we expect this book to do?

The purpose of the book is to create a broad perspective on the
main characteristics of leadership by illustrating how effective
leadership influences outcomes.

We envision a diversified audience across disciplines and occupa-
tions and with varying levels of experience and insight.

Successful outcomes achieved by reading this book include better
awareness and insight into planning for and evaluating leadership in a variety of settings.

Among those who can benefit from this document will be new
department heads and chairpersons, research leaders in academia and government, individuals in agricultural commodity
and trade associations and organizations, new industrial leaders, and perhaps consultants on leadership in agriculture. This
book also provides a basis for introductory courses in leadership, especially within an agricultural curriculum.

We address the inherent traits of leadership—both natural and
acquired:

What are the fundamental building blocks of leadership?
How does leadership emerge?
What promotes and provokes leadership behavior?
What can be taught and what is inherent?

Armed with these basic items, we identified the key elements in the
development of leadership and provided guideposts on how others
have led agricultural organizations and individuals to achieve success.

Where Can Leadership Be Manifested?

Leadership often shows itself in the launching of new thrusts, changes in institutional direction or priorities, or the consolidation of organizational units.

Leadership is also revealed in the assurance of consistent performances within an organization in not allowing a deadening of sensitivity or appreciation of what should be done in terms of quality, timeliness, and alertness relative to when items need to be accomplished.

Leadership is particularly critical in addressing crises, especially where programs, facilities, money, and people are all affected.

Leadership is especially needed in the development of the next generation of leaders. This is true in the production, processing, and distribution of agricultural products both within the industry and in government and academia.

We draw on a wide range of our experiences in various institutional settings to illustrate how the institutional backdrop shapes the emergence of leadership:

military
political
business/private sector
academic
international
What are the common features?

These issues are all addressed in this book, along with a thorough definition of leadership as it relates to agriculture.

What Is the Approach We Have Selected?

We have chosen to first address key factors in leadership in a narrative chapter, which at the same time reflects much of the history of leadership within agriculture. This is followed by a chapter addressing the critical issue of *character*, without which leadership cannot succeed.

The approach is fleshed out with a series of case studies that will give the reader background on a wide range of leadership challenges. These will be helpful to those who are successfully pursuing growth in a leadership capacity and will be useful to those in higher-echelon positions at all agricultural leadership levels. Finally, the case studies contain examples of both leadership successes and failures (or at least deficiencies) and reflect principles outlined in the first two chapters.

What Can We Learn from Others' Work and Case Studies?

The penultimate chapter, which is a synopsis of the book's key points, is followed by a chapter that provides suggestions on using this book in the developing and training of leaders.

References

Specific references on presented points are provided. Additionally, general references from the leadership literature may be especially useful to those who desire to study the subject in greater depth.

Appendixes

Three examples of structures for and approaches to approving re-search are provided for readers who are not familiar with certain parts of the agriculture system: universities, federal agencies (using the Agricultural Research Services [ARS] as the example), and industrial organizations.

Acknowledgments

Acknowledgements and thanks are due to many hands that have helped in the preparation of *Leadership in Agriculture: Case Studies for a New Generation,* including Leanne Chafin and Evelyn Folds (University of Georgia); Louise Jordan, who did splendid work in preparing the manuscript; David Songstad and Tamara Craig Shilling (Monsanto Corporation) and Charles E. Hess (University of California–Davis), who provided parts of the case studies; and several individuals who provided technical backup, especially in data and background. Special thanks go to Eric Young, Dan Rossi, Arlen Leholm, and Mike Harrington, who are executive directors for the four regions of the State Agricultural Experiment Stations, and also to T. E. Cleveland (USDA-ARS), who provided information on the project-review system of the USDA Agricultural Research Service. Also, we thank Clarence F. Davan Jr. (consultant) and Tamara Craig Shilling (Monsanto), who did the same with respect to the industrial approaches to project selection in appendix C.

Particular appreciation goes to Barry Jones (University of Georgia, retired editor) for tackling the major job of editing the volume. He influenced the design of the manuscript as well. The challenging task of ensuring that all of the pieces and edits were properly placed was skillfully undertaken by Betty Hoogerwerf (USDA-ARS, retired executive assistant).

Most of all we express our appreciation to our colleagues, with whom we have served over the years on government, university, and industrial assignments, all of which provided the milieu in which we as authors learned so much.

Leadership in Agriculture

Leadership in the Agricultural Environment

Evolution of Agriculture

During the last ten thousand years, a number of major developments have created evolutionary and revolutionary changes in the initial and simple concept of agriculture. From the nomadic hunter-gatherer lifestyle[1] to today's global environment, feeding the population has changed dramatically. As with any evolutionary process, some changes have been slow and methodical, while others have been much more rapid and episodic.[2]

In the history of agriculture, initial improvements were slow and incremental for the first few thousand years. A farmer in ancient Egypt four thousand years ago would probably feel very much at home in a European farmyard in the year AD 1500, an interval of thirty-five hundred years. Crude, man-powered farm implements, such as the moldboard plow, followed by the harnessing of animals, provided the additional muscle power that produced the first truly revolutionary change in agricultural production in the Western world. Another important change occurred in this early period when human beings discovered the means of preserving food by salting, drying, or smoking various commodities.

Each evolutionary step in the progression of agriculture called for critical leadership; one might even think in terms of inspired leadership. For example, in the beginning of this country, the early settlers worked with each other and with Native Americans to bring about a harvest. Almost every part of the country had some unique challenges that had to be overcome before agriculture could prosper. The Midwest required sturdier cultivation tools, which led to the development of the steel plow to till the region's heavy soils. Also, much of this potentially highly productive soil required drainage. In the South, much of the area was covered with pine forests, which had to be cleared before agriculture could be developed. While the timber was harvested and sold, the remaining fat pine stumps persisted. In fact, it was not until after World War II that many southern fields were free of the original forest remnants. In the West, the challenges were of a different sort but called for leadership in developing water sources and irrigation methods. Indeed, as agriculture emerged in each section of the country, a need for creative leadership also arose to deal with the challenges that limited agricultural production. This need has not abated. The challenge for greater agricultural productivity inspired Dr. Norman Borlaug and others to foster the "green revolution," which reflects a truly remarkable degree of inspired leadership.

In the seventeenth and eighteenth centuries, a series of incremental developments enhanced agricultural productivity.[3] With rapid population growth, the requirement for more food prompted farmers to grow more crops and livestock, and the use of horses and oxen provided more power for working the land. A steady improvement in tools such as the cradle (to hold grain, etc.) and the scythe also increased farm productivity. With the invention of the cotton gin in 1793, preparing cotton for market became much more efficient, providing a cash crop for a new, fledgling United States. To encourage the growth of agriculture in these early years as a nation, land was plentiful and available free or at minimal cost, as evidenced in the Homestead Act.

As the nineteenth century was drawing to a close, the advent of mechanization in agriculture brought about other startling and revolutionary changes. The invention of the internal combustion engine allowed gasoline and electrically generated power to replace the muscle power of both man and beast. In the latter part of the twentieth century, as these devices were developed further, they were incorporated into a great variety of agricultural processes, producing yet another revolution in the production of foodstuffs.

The twentieth century also brought crop (especially corn) hybridization and the introduction of agrochemicals. Toward the end of the century the science of biotechnology, which created new and more useful food crops, gained a foothold. These advancements dramatically increased crop yields for the average farmer by allowing food grown by fewer individuals to be used to feed the world's increasing population.

As the twenty-first century proceeds, agriculture is expanding its traditional portfolio. In the past, agriculture provided food for humans, feed for livestock and poultry, and agronomic and horticultural crops, and also met fiber needs. Now added to these traditional expectations is a demand for farmers to produce biomass, which can be converted into an energy source and many other valuable bioproducts. This new requirement is driven by a world that desires a greater degree of sustainable and secure energy. By using biotechnology and various genetic modifications, crop plants can produce unique components that also have medicinal and other health-improving properties. Humankind appears to be on the cusp of another agricultural revolution that may change the face of this endeavor in as yet unimaginable ways.

However, these changes are accompanied by certain costs. An excellent example is the influence of grain prices, especially those of corn, which have an impact on the "finishing" or fattening of cattle. High corn prices spell trouble for the feedlot owner, whereas low corn prices make the feedlot owner happy. In the energy story, we need to see how increasing use of crops for energy can have a marginal effect on food prices. Tradeoffs are important.

Human history documents well that the evolution and development of civilization has closely paralleled agricultural development.

During the earliest "hunter-gatherer era," agricultural output was finite, limited by what one man or woman could kill or gather. However, as agriculture has developed, it has become increasingly sustainable and thus capable of providing sustenance for the world's ever-growing population. Today, the planet supports the needs of seven billion people, a number that is projected to grow to nine billion by mid-century.[4] Compounding the demand further, many of these people will live much longer than their ancient ancestors. Additionally, as a major result of the success of agriculture, an increasing portion of our population has been freed up to follow other pursuits. Thus, as a greater portion of the population is able to disengage from the essential process of food production, more people are able to build and advance civilization.

The Need for Leadership

As agriculture has evolved, its complexity has increased and now involves the basic sciences, engineering, and economics. There is a growing need for leadership to keep all aspects of the agricultural portfolio working in harmony. While some facets of our economy are fraught with problems and concerns about the loss of competitiveness, agriculture in the United States has been and remains highly successful. Our contention is that, in this rapidly changing environment, *effective leadership* is vitally important to maintain agriculture's continued success.

One of the early efforts in producing effective leadership involved the land-grant institutions, colleges (now universities) created by Congress to educate the citizenry in the increasingly complex field of agriculture during the latter half of the nineteenth century and throughout the twentieth. See appendix A for details about the system.

In the mid-1800s, the vast majority of Americans farmed. Thus there was a need to (1) educate students, (2) utilize science to increase agricultural productivity, and (3) ensure that citizens received the benefit of such efforts. The Morrill Act of 1862 established college-level efforts to educate young students in the field of agriculture; the Hatch Act of 1887 focused on employing science to stimulate agricultural production; and a series of other federal acts strengthened this outreach effort for forestry, animal health, and so on.

When more pieces of the "new knowledge" were added, the need for leadership to bring the results of these innovations to the agricultural community (i.e., those producers, processors, distributors, and providers of support services such as transportation and banking—in effect an ever-increasing agricultural industry) became clear. With the evolution of the system, directors, department heads, and deans were brought into the picture. Particularly evident in more recent times was the bringing together of the three basic units—academia, research, and outreach/extension—as an integrated system with the corresponding centralization of institutional leadership vested in a single senior administrator. At the institutional level, this development was strengthened by a corresponding integration of the three missions and quickly involved the industrial component of agriculture as a source of advice.

In larger institutions, the earlier amalgamation of a dean's or a vice president's responsibilities with those of the directors of the experiment stations and extension services has tended to be so unwieldy that a devolution of leadership and responsibility is now occurring. Directors of the experiment stations and extension services now function as chief operating officers who often report to a central leader (dean, vice president, vice provost, etc.) rather than having all of these titles vested in one person. Parallel stories from industrial organizations tend to show the same need for leadership and various patterns of organization.

James MacGregor Burns, a noted scholar of leadership studies, has observed that "leadership is one of the most observed and least understood phenomena on earth."[5] Despite this, leadership is omnipresent in human society, and, as Bernard Bass observes, "Leadership occurs universally among all people regardless of culture."[6] As agriculture grew in size, complexity, and economic status in the last two centuries, it clearly required effective leadership and an attendant structure. The complex overall model for food and agriculture has become ever more interconnected but is still made up of individual building blocks. To function effectively the parts must work well together. In the integrated model for agriculture in contemporary times, both individual and shared *leadership are now more essential than ever for success.*

Operational Aspects of Leadership and Organization

Despite a common need for leadership, the challenge in agriculture is nevertheless diverse, owing to the special nature of agriculture itself. For the present purposes, however, we may consider leadership in agriculture in several distinct areas: (1) support for research and education; (2) production and harvesting in farming and ranching; (3) commodity and trade; (4) marketing and processing; and (5) distribution, use, and sale of agricultural commodities.

Support for Research, Education, and Extension
Factors contributing to the success of agriculture in the United States include a wealth of good soil, a favorable climate and geography, abundant or at least adequate water, good transportation, an effective communication systems, a generally favorable regulatory climate, a viable banking and financial system, and highly skilled farmers. Indeed, one the greatest contributors to this success is the unique research, education, and extension system, which provides a constant infusion of innovative operators, as well as new information, knowledge, and technology pertaining to agriculture.

Thus, the agricultural system needs aggressive and effective leadership. This simple fact was recognized a number of years ago and is described in great detail in the "Enhancing Leadership in the State Agricultural Experiment Stations" case study in this book, which describes a very useful teaching tool. In fact, many of the graduates of this program have been able to secure leadership jobs in the agricultural research, education, and extension system. On the other hand, some would argue that success has been elusive because financial support for the system has not kept pace with its needs. Parallel pictures can be found in governmental agriculture. Funding for agricultural research and outreach is constantly under scrutiny by legislators. Consequently, there is a critical need for leaders who can direct change to keep these programs relevant.

Production and Harvesting

The most basic and visible aspect of agriculture is the actual growing and harvesting of crops and the production of livestock. Recognizing a need for enhanced management in these areas, several states have implemented leadership-development programs focusing on young farmers, agribusiness personnel, and others involved in various aspects of agricultural enterprises. The Kellogg Foundation,[7] long a supporter of leadership enhancement in all endeavors, has backed these state agricultural leadership programs—with remarkable results. In several states, graduates of such programs have achieved great success in their communities. Among other accomplishments they have become members of the state legislature and even served as the agriculture liaison to the governor. In Georgia, for example, before taking part in the program, one individual, whose interests had previously ended literally at the fence that surrounded his tobacco farm, found that the leadership program gave him a new perspective. As a result, he became a key person on the staff that advised Georgia's governor and his administration on agricultural matters.

Commodity and Trade

One of agriculture's strengths in the United States is the strong commitment to developing trade relations with other countries. The consistently favorable balance of trade in agricultural commodities can be traced primarily to the strong commodity management of organizations such as the National Cotton Council and the American Sugar Cane League. Some have been successful, and others have not. These organizations work from numerous perspectives, including political policy, and also seek to develop standard rules and regulations to foster enhanced trade among nations. Through specific acts and, more recently, the US Farm Bill (beginning in the last quarter of the twentieth century), the price of sugar, for example, in the United States has remained relatively constant while world prices have fluctuated.

Processing, Marketing, and Sales

Clearly a vital step in the agricultural enterprise is the processing, marketing, and sale of agricultural products, a complex area in which success is highly contingent on its effectiveness. Because the processing and marketing of agricultural products involve working with the corporate world, it is quite common for individuals in such enterprises to receive leadership training from the corporate sector. Nevertheless, the unique aspects of agriculture require that these individuals have an appreciation of all the components involved in its success.

Distribution, Use, and Safety

The final component of the agricultural enterprise is distribution and use, the importance of which is difficult to overestimate. Those in the Western world, and especially in the United States, have a moral responsibility to ensure that all humankind is nourished. This is no small task, as we in this country who have worked with disaster relief, welfare relief, food banks, and many other programs (including the food stamp program; nutrition programs for women, infants, and children; and school lunch programs) have learned. In addition, in the use of food, the issue of safety is paramount. Although the United States has a safe food supply, a number of people die each year because of tainted food, and we experience a small but steady stream of food-product recalls that often narrowly avert a disaster.

Functional Leadership in the Operations

Leadership involves the identification and acquisition of resources for a particular group or endeavor, a function that is rapidly growing in importance in today's environment. As the need for visionary guidance is becoming increasingly critical in the identification of research and education priorities, one of the major challenges is securing funding from various levels of government and from private sources since everyone benefits from this effort. As competition for scarce resources becomes more intense, this will be an increasingly difficult challenge that calls for innovative and inspired direction.

Although there are significant problems in agriculture today, many more are becoming apparent as we move into the future. Issues such as genetically modified organisms (GMOs) vs. non-GMOs, organic vs. conventional production, caged or free-range chicken and egg production, food vs. fuel production using agricultural crops must be considered. All of these pose a challenge because they are highly emotional matters that involve moral issues and political considerations. Also looming on the horizon is opposition to animal agriculture. Negotiating these challenges will require exceedingly skilled leadership. Shared leadership from the various elements of an integrated industry will be required to conceive, develop, and market a working vision for the future. Put together with individual leadership, this would ensure an effective combination of sound economic, environmental, and general welfare aspects in modern agricultural systems.

The areas of processing, marketing, and sales are exceedingly critical because their success ensures that of the total agricultural enterprise. The biggest challenge here is ensuring that individuals can easily move between components of the agricultural enterprise, which calls for the utmost in skilled leadership.

Crucial Pathways

Several crucial parallel pathways affecting food and agriculture have emerged in our nation's relatively short history, increasing rapidly across time at often exponential rates. Taken together, the resulting growth and maturation of the food and agriculture system have driven demands for increased sophistication of its leadership. Individual leadership down to the farm level is still critical, while many of these parallel pathways intersect and create new and complex forms of shared leadership that operate on a continuum of scale from local to global. The following are illustrative of the intersecting changes that continue to drive the need for effective direction:

Geographic growth of the agricultural enterprise with settlement of new lands in the early history of our country

Growth from subsistence farming and ranching to larger commercial enterprises both nationally and internationally

Development of the multidimensional national infrastructure supporting the industrial revolution

Increasing global demand for food, fiber, fuel, and other agricultural products

Evolution of knowledge—the rapid expansion of science and its products that fueled the industrial revolution in agriculture and that is now fueling a revolution in biology, information technology, and modern applications of computational capacities

Increasing sophistication of the academic research, extension, and education system, as well as governmental agencies that continue to evolve to support changing citizen needs while

coping with complexity in the parallel evolution of the food
and agriculture enterprise

Evolution from relatively simple individual farms and ranches to
larger distributed operations with a mandate for broader and
more sophisticated capacities to operate in the global "village"

A requirement for increasingly visionary and sophisticated leadership to enable the food and agriculture system to function
effectively in the larger, evolving industrial system

Evolution of Leadership

At the dawn of civilization, the survival of humankind depended on
the collective actions of hunter-gatherers to acquire and share food.
Early leadership must have emerged to organize and direct these collective actions.

Oral and written history on food and agriculture has captured and
transmitted experience and wisdom from one generation to the next.
This represents the earliest and a continuing basis for leadership in
education, where leaders were the guardians of history. Even in less
developed countries today, "farmer wisdom" transferred orally from
one generation to another is still regarded as a critical component
of production systems that affect both institutional and individual
behavior.

Transition from subsistence farming that feeds one family to com-
munity- and market-based production systems, where farmers produce enough to feed an increasingly larger number of nonfarming
populations, has resulted in the emergence of more complex systems
that include producing, transporting, processing, and marketing.
This has been led by the creation of new and more specialized leaders
for both the individual components and the aggregate food system.
Food and agriculture management is interwoven with leadership of
the broader societal fabric, which continues as an "expanding uni-
verse" over time.

What has driven the evolution of agricultural leadership historically? What is its relation to the more complex societies as they become increasingly interdependent? Most important, what lessons does history teach us about future leadership in the complex food and agriculture system? But the real question is, *How, in the twenty-first century, are we going to successfully feed, clothe, and house a rapidly growing global population?*

What characteristics must leaders have if they are to meet such
needs?
How do we go about developing such leaders in industry, government, and academia?
Are there examples of successes and failures in agricultural
leadership that will help us see what can and should be done?
How will we know whether we have succeeded or failed?

This book is designed to address such questions using specific case studies and examples. Agriculture is clearly our most important enterprise for the continued life of humankind on this planet. Consequently, it will depend upon the emergence of more effective leadership if it is to move forward.

Character

THE BEDROCK OF LEADERS AND LEADERSHIP

Character is the bedrock on which the whole edifice of leadership rests. It is the prime element for which every profession, every corporation, every industry searches in evaluating a member of its organization. With it, the full worth of an individual can be developed. Without it . . . mediocrity . . . will result.

Gen. Matthew B. Ridgway

Introduction

Character is as essential to a leader as oxygen is to respiration. With respect to leadership, the importance of character is highlighted by examining the definition adopted. In this work, leadership is defined as the act and process of inspiring others to participate in an endeavor oriented in a specific direction and/or intended to accomplish a particular objective.

Since any leadership situation requires the existence of at least two individuals (which thus distinguishes it from individual personal achievement), the statement establishes and emphasizes an essential leadership component: associating and working with others. Leadership is intrinsically communal in nature and is also a relationship among participants and collaborators. In addition, it is an inherently active and positive force to achieve beneficial results, meaning that it involves getting the right things done in the right way and at the right time.

By characterizing leadership in this manner—as an act, a process, and a relationship—it is clear that successful leaders must have vision (i.e., an ability to put ideas into action to achieve results); courage to deal with conflict about an intended direction or goal; an ability to inspire others to want to be a part of that common direction; and the capacity to build teams or bring others into a particular endeavor.

It is also apparent that character and the ability to recognize and "do good" (i.e., get the right things done in the right way and at the right time) are paramount to this definition and essential to its understanding and successful implementation.

"Character" can be a "loaded" term in today's society, so it is important to present a precise definition to establish what it means in the context of this book: Character is the combination of qualities distinguishing an individual person from a moral-ethical perspective. It guides one's decisions and actions. In essence, character is the sum total of an individual's personality traits and the link between that person's values and behavior.

An individual's success as a leader is influenced by several factors, especially character. Accordingly, successful leaders are constantly searching for ways to enhance their effectiveness, building on strengths and striving to minimize weaknesses. Character helps enhance effectiveness. Certain character aspects are somewhat innate, while other elements may be developed, strengthened, or enhanced over time with deliberate practice. "All human virtues increase and strengthen themselves by the practice and experience of them," Socrates wrote. He indicated that virtues are neither immutable nor permanent.

Building on this statement, it follows that although all "human virtues" are valuable, some are essential, and others, although not essential, are nonetheless important for leaders. Focusing on essential and desirable virtues is the approach employed here. Essential virtues are "cardinal virtues," while important virtues fall into three categories: thinking, acting, and believing. Figure 1 illustrates this model.

The Cardinal Virtues

These essential virtues are known as the "cardinal virtues" ("cardinal" derives from the Latin word *cardo*, meaning "hinge"). They are identified by this term because they are the wellsprings from which all other moral and ethical traits emanate and thus serve as the "hinges" or axes upon which morality pivots. Effective leaders must possess and manifest these four virtues. The four traditional cardinal virtues (and their modern counterparts) are Prudence (Wisdom), Justice, Temperance (Moderation), and Fortitude (Courage).

Prudence
Prudence is defined as the ability to judge among choices in order to take the appropriate actions at a given time. It is listed first because it is considered a "rudder" virtue, which "steers" all of the other virtues.[1] While the contemporary connotation of prudence suggests excessive caution, and it has largely been supplanted in the list of cardinal virtues by its modern cousin, "wisdom," the decision to include "prudence" instead of "wisdom" is deliberate.

The etymology of the word "prudence" indicates that it refers to "wisdom gained through experience" as opposed to study. Thus, "practical wisdom" is the precise meaning we desire. Aristotle maintained that "it is impossible to be good in the full sense of the word without practical wisdom or to be a man of practical wisdom without moral excellence or virtue."[2] Because prudence helps a leader determine right from wrong, it is an essential virtue. "Prudence not only helps us be of good counsel, but also [helps us] to judge and [lead] well," St. Thomas Aquinas wrote.[3]

Judgment, the outward manifestation of prudence, is one of the most important traits of character that define an individual. Sound judgment ensures that a mature individual makes decisions that are based on the best information and evidence available. Such deci-

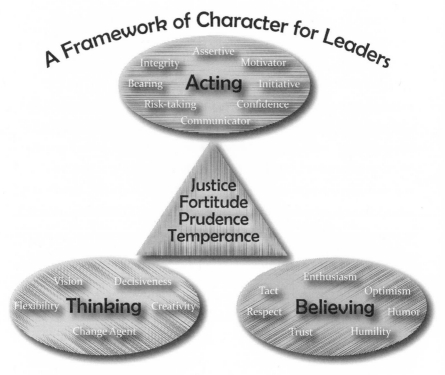

Figure 1. A Framework of Character for Leaders.

sions are not emotional responses; rather, they are carefully thought through and made in a methodical and deliberate manner. Those who use sound judgment always consider how their decisions and actions influence the big picture and other people.

Severe budget problems often offer an excellent opportunity to observe leaders who exhibit (or fail to exhibit) sound judgment. In carrying out a reduction in force (RIF), one of us found it easy to let legal boundaries guide the process:

> I recall one such situation where I was the responsible person, and I had done my homework—legally speaking. Fortunately, I had some staff members who were able to offer different approaches

that accomplished the RIF. My staff searched diligently to discover new opportunities in which individuals that were already scheduled to be terminated were able to be reassigned or relocated. We were mostly successful, and our efforts were quickly recognized. Although my rush to judgment was poorly conceived, the persistent strength of my staff carried the day, and in the end, it was a win-win situation.

Another incident occurred when one of us was very young. It reflected the extremely poor judgment of one man and demonstrated the sound judgment of another:

We needed to purchase some tobacco sticks. My father learned of a neighbor's desire to sell some of his sticks, so my father made arrangements to purchase a thousand sticks from this neighbor. We used the sticks and, in the process, mixed the recently purchased sticks with our original sticks. About three years after the purchase of the sticks, the neighbor came to our house early one morning and told my father he had the money and wanted to buy back "his" sticks. At the busiest time of the year on a tobacco farm, my father's consternation was great.

After a lengthy discussion, my father announced that we would start that afternoon going through some five thousand tobacco sticks to try to locate the particular thousand we had purchased from the neighbor. That night I asked my father why we had returned the neighbor's sticks. My father replied that he offered him new sticks, but the man had said he wanted his own, original sticks back. My father acquiesced because this farmer had a reputation for settling his disagreements with fire. My father figured a few hours' work picking out the neighbor's sticks was a good insurance policy. This illustrates an almost total lack of good judgment on the part of one farmer and quite sound judgment from my father (even though at the time I thought he was being foolish).

Justice

Justice, the next most important virtue, is the ability to discern properly between one's own rights and needs and those of others. Stated differently, justice is "giving everyone his [or her] due."[4] While the word itself may not convey its full meaning as a cardinal virtue, it is nonetheless essential because, when duties conflict, leaders must use the elements of justice and prudence to discern what best satisfies all of their obligations. In practical terms, justice allows leaders to gain perspective on the competing demands in order to make optimal decisions.

No matter what the area in agriculture, the treatment of all people in a fair and honorable manner is important. Regardless of race, religion, color, sex, age, national origin, or region in the country from which a person comes, everyone should be treated fairly. A successful leader must not only treat all people fairly but must also ensure that justice prevails throughout the organization. This is a primary responsibility of every leader, regardless of position.

Temperance

Temperance refers to restraint, self-discipline, and self-control; those who practice temperance prioritize responsibility over desires and obey their will instead of their instinct. The Greeks equated temperance with being "of sound mind." Aristotle conceived of temperance as "the mean between excess and defect."[5] Its modern derivation is "moderation," which has a similar meaning but emphasizes "restricting" over restraint and is thus an acceptable alternative but is not entirely interchangeable as a precise term. In just this vein, La Rochefoucauld wrote that "moderation is an ostentatious proof of our strength of character."

The practice of temperance helps people to recognize and accept the limitations of acceptable action and to choose among available alternatives. It also helps one reconcile the inevitable conflicts between personal morality and professional ethics, between responsibilities and expectations. Temperate leaders act in the best interest of others rather than themselves and make decisions that utilize the *acceptable* choices available; doing so ensures that they are first and foremost good human beings.

One vital aspect of temperance is self-discipline. Before one can lead or have any influence on others, one must exhibit self-control, which means being able to control one's emotions as well as actions. In leadership situations, one must at times show disapproval in a strong way; however, it should always be done in a controlled manner. The leader who exercises self-discipline is dependable and is a positive influence in a disciplined organization.

In agriculture, few issues are as highly charged emotionally as animal confinement, use of pesticides, and genetically modified organisms (GMOs). Dealing with these issues at all levels requires that we have strong self-discipline and maintain our composure even when under great stress. To be successful, we need to "keep our cool." Let others lose their heads; that will provide an excellent opportunity to gain an advantage.

Athletics provides excellent examples of these traits as well. For example, some football coaches are virtually sideshows at competitive games. They jump around, pull their hair, curse, and exhibit other antics that more befit a kindergartener. On the other hand, some coaches are pillars of strength. One of those remembered for his temperate demeanor on the field is the late Tom Landry, former coach of the Dallas Cowboys, a professional football team.

Fortitude

Finally, *fortitude* encompasses the traits of forbearance, endurance, perseverance, and the ability and willingness to confront fear, uncertainty, and/or intimidation. Fortitude is more expansive than courage, which is generally limited to the notions of incidental bravery and audacity. It is broader in that it may refer to physical or moral aspects; it addresses both physical and moral bravery and includes the characteristics of stamina, resilience, and restraint (forbearance), making it a much better choice for inclusion among the cardinal virtues.

The ancients believed that the best way to become a good person was to act correctly, which in time would establish precedence and habit and allow a person to become better through the repetition of good acts. According to one modern author, fortitude "is character in action; it is a pattern; it is a settled disposition (a habitus) formed, fashioned, and developed over many years," echoing the beliefs of the ancients and providing a solid foundation for its inclusion with the other three cardinal virtues.[6] Without action, which is an essential component of this work's definition, leadership cannot occur. Fortitude provides leaders with the ability and willingness to act as they should both consistently and predictably, providing the essential component of action to the elements encompassed by the other three cardinal virtues.

One aspect of fortitude is perseverance, which reflects commitment, patience, and a willingness to try repeatedly. One of the authors of this book has seen farmers plant cotton three or four times before getting a good stand. This can happen in a cold, wet spring coupled with low-quality seed.

In the political process, identifying farm-friendly legislation requires strong perseverance sometimes coupled with new legislation or changing times. Agricultural leaders must be willing to work and persevere until there is overwhelming evidence that another course is needed. Napoleon Bonaparte once said, "Victory belongs to the most persevering."

Perseverance enables us to accomplish goals we had thought impossible. Getting successfully through army basic training or completing all of the requirements for a PhD are two challenges that require perseverance. A successful leader stays with a project or an effort long after doing simply what is expected or minimally acceptable.

Nobel laureate Norman Borlaug's effort is a classic example of perseverance. Borlaug had an idea of how to shorten the time it took to breed new wheat varieties. By combining his determined efforts with staying the course, he convinced administrators to allow him to use a novel breeding approach that resulted in substantially reducing the time to breed new wheat cultivars. His perseverance paid off in the end, and his success played a key role in the "green revolution."

Thomas Edison is another classic example of perseverance. Many of Edison's inventions did not at first work, but he persevered. Upon reflecting on his failures, he said, "I have not failed. I just found 10,000 ways that won't work." Edison is also credited with saying that success requires 10 percent inspiration and 90 percent perspiration.

"The difference between a hero and a coward is [that] the hero fights five minutes longer!" Napoleon said. Perseverance wins the day.

Another aspect of fortitude is endurance, which may be thought of as similar to perseverance; however, it differs in that the "endurance" of an individual fosters perseverance in other people and organizations. Endurance flows out of commitment and leads to perseverance. When things are going well, it is easy to endure hot weather or harsh conditions. One of the authors, while serving as an experiment station director, recalls a year when an ice storm hit and knocked out the power at the station dairy late on a Friday afternoon.

After a few hours we were told by the power company that there was no hope for restored power for at least two days. High-producing dairy cows simply must be milked. Concerned, I drove out to the dairy on Saturday morning. When I arrived, I was not surprised to see the milkers and most of the departmental physical-plant technicians working on an old diesel generator while others were putting up wind protectors. What did surprise me was that the department head and most of the departmental professors, even the nondairy faculty, were there as well. Of course, I could not leave until the generator was running and the cows were being milked. Admittedly, the department head, departmental professors, and I contributed little to solving the problem, but our presence made the workers feel better because their "bosses" were enduring the cold with them—even if we were of little use!

The Essentiality of the Cardinal Virtues

Cardinal virtues are essential for leaders to possess and demonstrate routinely and repeatedly. Evidence from the ancients illustrates the necessity of being both good human beings and good leaders. The abilities encompassed by Prudence, Justice, Temperance, and Fortitude represent the foundation from which leaders may be developed and from which they must operate. As the derivation of the word "cardinal" indicates, the absence of any one of these characteristics results in an individual with a flawed character who will be unable to rise to the status of the truly successful leader.

Important Character Attributes to Be Acquired and Developed

The successful leader in agriculture needs both the essential character traits identified as cardinal virtues and considerable strengths in other areas, including "thinking," "acting," and "believing" and their associated attributes. The absence of strength and capability in any of these areas and/or their associated attributes is characterized neither as a character flaw nor as detrimental as it is with respect to the cardinal virtues. This is because deficiencies in these areas can be overcome, and attributes can be acquired and developed if individuals are aware of their deficiencies and work to compensate for them. They must be aware of their character, recognizing strong points and areas that must be strengthened. This essential aspect of leadership must be an ongoing process.

Thinking

Thinking addresses the leader's intellectual abilities. A leader's intellect encompasses the application of intelligent judgment and includes the attributes of vision, decisiveness, flexibility, and creativity, as well as the ability to function as a change agent. An in-depth description of each attribute follows.

An ability to conceive, develop, and communicate a vision to people in an organization is perhaps the most important character attribute of a leader. Successful leaders must have a clear vision of where they want to go or take an organization/group. They must be able to convey an idealized description of the expected outcome of the efforts of others or for an organization.

The establishment of the research hypothesis is an act of conceptualizing a problem and developing possible outcomes in the research process. In agriculture, vision often is that of the leadership of an organization or group rather than of an individual. The effort of the Experiment Station Committee on Policy (ESCOP) to initiate a leadership development program, the creation of the Council for Agriculture Science and Technology (CAST) by a few individuals representing several scientific societies, and the development of the National Research Initiative (NRI) in the USDA Cooperative State Research Education and Extension Service (CSREES) a few years ago are all excellent examples of visioning. These were all visionary undertakings that enjoyed a reasonable degree of collective support. Each of these efforts is described in greater detail in the case studies. However, the point is that great accomplishments begin with the vision of a single individual.

A successful leader has to be decisive, that is, able to fully understand the decision-making process and willing to make decisions in a timely fashion. Anyone can be decisive, but an effective leader who is decisive knows how to collect the facts, consider the options, and regularly make the best decision within the given circumstances.

Understanding the decision-making process is essential. In the book *Applied Logic,* Little, Wilson, and Moore point out several subjective irrelevancies in the decision-making process.[7] One, "decision by indecision," explains how failure to make a decision is, in essence, making a decision. For example, deciding on a candidate for an important faculty position requires doing the proper "homework" and then making a decision. However, not reaching a decision is, indeed, also a decision. On the farm, there are countless situations where decisiveness is important. For example, before planting a crop, the farmer must decide about contracting the crop. Failure to do so means the farmer must accept the prevailing price of the commodity at time of harvest.

Flexibility. The successful person always has a Plan B when Plan A does not work. When the situation changes or new evidence becomes available, the successful leader will actively consider a different approach. At one time, one of the authors had a research technician who would challenge the author by saying, "If you want to screw it up, we'll do it your way, Doc." Much of the time this called for a critical reevaluation or reassessment on the author's part.

Effective leaders recognize that being flexible is not a sign of weakness. Rather, it is a highly desirable attribute that enables them to make the best of any situation.

Good leadership demands creativity. Successful leaders are constantly searching for a new idea or fresh approach. General George S. Patton, that great World War II leader, once said, "Never tell people *how* to do things; rather, tell them *what* to do, and they will surprise you with their ingenuity." What a thought!

A leader must "bring something to the table." However, never underestimate the ideas of subordinates. Even the slowest or most inexperienced person in a group sometimes has a great idea. The old axiom "Even a blind hog sometimes finds an acorn" has some truth. A leader must be intuitive enough to recognize good ideas and, of course, give credit to those who provide them.

A great challenge in agriculture is to sustain creativity in all areas. Sadly, agriculture has adversaries who are far more creative in attacking production agriculture than agricultural leaders are at responding to such attacks.

The role of the visionary leader inherently brings with it the need to be a change agent. Such a leader is often the first person to see the need for organizational change. "It is not the strongest of the species that survives or the most intelligent that survives. It is the one that is most adaptable to change," Charles Darwin so aptly pointed out. Thus, to resist change is to jeopardize survival. Consequently, an individual who sees a need for change and carries it out is reflecting the highest order of leadership. All facets of agriculture, from research to production, are dynamic, and having a leader who can effectively manage change helps ensure continued success.

A persistent reluctance to leave the comfort zone and avoid change unfortunately permeates agricultural enterprises that have been in place with only modest change since the Great Depression. This is a significant negative phenomenon for present and future agricultural leaders. In the agricultural sciences, there is a great tendency for scientists to work on projects of the greatest personal interest rather than those that will instead benefit institutions, industry, and society. In academia, new faculty members often want to continue their dissertation research. Within the research community, too, some individuals are reluctant to support funding mechanisms such as the competitive process, which is used in most areas of science. In each of these areas, agriculture is comfortable with the past and is not campaigning for change. However, as Darwin reminds us with respect to the animal kingdom, survival requires change and adaptation. This is no less true for many aspects of agriculture as well.

Acting

Acting involves a leader's physical abilities. It makes use of a leader's presence and actions, encompasses the things a leader does, and calls on the leader's integrity, initiative, risk-taking ability, communication skills, confidence, motivation, assertiveness, and bearing. An in-depth description of each attribute follows.

Integrity is honorable behavior, and it may also refer to consistency between one's beliefs and one's actions. A person without integrity is doomed to a life of failure as a leader.

An individual who possesses integrity is always honest and sincere, tells the truth, and lets the "chips fall where they may." The clincher, "one's word is one's bond" or "you can take (so-and-so's) word to the bank," describes a person with integrity in both senses. People with integrity never shade a point of view or cut any corners. Rather, they always give the full story, an honest interpretation as they see it, and act accordingly. Situations in which a lack of integrity becomes apparent are striking, and the following examples illustrate this point.

One of the authors remembers a graduate student who made an interesting observation about the specific effect of a particular herbicide on plants. It was not a major discovery, but it was an original observation on the herbicide's mode of action. "Imagine my surprise when an abstract of a paper was presented by a colleague at a scientific meeting outlining this observation by my student! He did not credit my student and, consequently, failed the test of integrity."

The same author observed another example of a lack of integrity when a farmer added extra sand to baskets of tobacco sand lugs at the local tobacco market. The sand lugs, which comprise the first priming of tobacco, are already sandy since they are the leaves that grow closer to the ground. Some farmers rationalize their participation in this practice by arguing that they are simply adding back some of the sand lost in processing the tobacco for curing. Sand at 75 to 80 cents per pound would strikingly enhance the farmer's bottom line. Occasionally, a skilled warehouseman would challenge a farmer when he suspected that the tobacco had been "sanded." It would take only one time for this practice to be revealed for a farmer to be branded for life as a person with no integrity.

A final example offered by the same author about a lack of integrity involved the practice of stimulating cows to gorge themselves on water just prior to crossing the scales at the local stockyard. This was often thought of as a harmless exercise. Of course, the extra water was soon lost. "I remember a group of farmers debating whether the water the cows drank weighed as much in the cow as it did in the water trough. Whether it had much effect on cattle weight was debatable, but it clearly demonstrated a lack of integrity with respect to obtaining accurate cattle weight."

Agricultural leaders must also demonstrate initiative. This is the attribute that enables a person to recognize a need for action and to bring it about. Without such resourcefulness, nothing happens. Of course, it is important that people recognize the impact of other attributes that help transform initiative from simply action for action's sake into efforts that get the right things done. It is not enough to simply display such ingenuity; it must also be focused and contribute toward accomplishing assigned goals in a timely fashion.

Displaying initiative is doing something when one could just as easily be justified in doing nothing at all. Early in my career, I was a member of a national organization that needed to make a personnel change in the paid executive position. The president of the organization was coming to the end of his term of office, and he could have easily been content to simply ride out his term as a lame duck, leaving the issue for his successor to act upon once he took office. This outgoing president, however, stepped up to the plate and decided to make a bold and difficult move.

While many years have passed, I still vividly recall the inventiveness demonstrated by this person, who went on to become president of one of our nation's leading universities. Clearly, he took the initiative when it would have been easier to just "kick the can down the road" and leave an unpleasant task for someone else. This incident provides an excellent example of a person who did not shirk his responsibility and instead took action when it was needed.

A successful leader must have a genuine appreciation for and an understanding of risk and be willing to take some calculated risks. Risk differs significantly from a gamble: one has a reasonable chance of success with and may recover from the former, but neither consequence is true for the latter. As such, risk-taking activities must be carefully assessed, be appropriate to the situation, and stand a reasonable chance of success. Having taken these factors into account, leaders must also know how much risk to take.

In addition, it is important to know when to take risk and when to be more conservative. Even more critical is knowing how to manage risk. There are few guarantees in life, and the old adage "nothing ventured, nothing gained" provides an appropriate justification for the potential of risk. Teaching farmers how to "forward contract" is an exceedingly difficult facet of the extension service's educational portfolio. In managing risk, there are no guarantees.

Other character attributes have an element of risk associated with them. For example, both initiative and decisiveness are inherently driven by a willingness to accept risks. The successful leader realizes that these highly desirable attributes may pave the way for failure or success, but that person is always several jumps ahead when taking risks such that when things go sour, there are alternative paths to success.

Effective communication is absolutely necessary for successful leadership. It is not enough that people hear you; they must understand you as well. Successful leaders also hear and understand those they are leading. They listen carefully and communicate their message effectively. They should also give their undivided attention to those with whom they are talking. Have you ever been talking to someone and noticed that the person was scanning the room for a more prestigious partner to converse with? That is an example of poor communication.

As an administrator, one of the authors of this book often had to listen to subordinates complain about meetings: "In fact, most of us have complained about spending too much of our time in meetings. However, I am confident that not knowing what is going on and being uninformed would invoke far more complaints than complaining about too many meetings."

Confidence allows successful leaders not only to know where they want to go but also to instill their confidence in others in order to accomplish their shared objectives together. Confidence enhances a leader's opportunity to be successful. Even when the outcome is uncertain, confidence conveys that the leader always has alternative solutions whenever needed.

As a scientist and an administrator over the years, one of the authors of this book observed extension service professionals while they worked. Invariably, those specialists who conveyed confidence in their recommendations were the most successful. Certainly pesticide salespersons must also have confidence in the products they are selling.

Confidence is contagious, and leaders who exhibit self-confidence inspire individuals throughout their organization to think with more assurance. Their manner tends to help eliminate doubt. Confidence is derived through competence. It is difficult, if not impossible, for leaders to be confident when they do not know their job.

No leader can achieve his or her goals acting alone, so the ability to motivate others is an important leadership quality. Getting an entire team to pull in the same direction is challenging, and this is done through motivation. Besides providing groups with purpose and direction, a leader's most important contribution to a project may well be inspiring others and providing motivation to the process. There are as many approaches to motivation as there are individuals. The successful leader quickly learns many ways to motivate individuals effectively and employs the most effective approach in each situation.

The leader who is a successful motivator is one who can inspire others and instill a desire in the members of the team to excel. Force alone is seldom a satisfactory approach, and while shame and embarrassment work on occasion, the best way to induce the team's best efforts is to inspire them to strive for excellence and to motivate them to action.

One of the authors once asked faculty members to prepare summaries of the impact of their programs for the previous year. As expected, the response was poor. "I then let it be known that no one had to submit a response. However, in lieu of a response they simply had to send a statement indicating that their program did not have any discernible impact in the previous year. Again, as expected, I soon had excellent responses to the original request."

A successful leader must have a reasonable degree of assertiveness. This is one attribute that can easily be overdone, as its "shadow" can be detrimental. The successful leader must know the degree of assertiveness necessary for success. A lack of assertiveness means that jobs never get done, whereas being overly assertive may cause a leader to lose critical support and reduce the opportunity for success.

What is the right degree of assertiveness to use? Enough to enable one to speak up and to ensure that one's ideas are considered. Insisting on one's point of view and disregarding the opinions of others can cause friction; as a result, others may view a leader as overly aggressive. Observations of panel moderators reveal that good ones ensure that those who are reticent to speak are encouraged to contribute because they know that these people sometimes have excellent ideas. In addition, of course, some panel members talk all the time and never say anything worthwhile. The key is to moderate the degree, timing, and intensity of participation.

Maintaining a proper bearing—how one moves or stands—tells the world a leader is in control. Successful leaders learn how to control their emotions and body language. Bearing is situational, meaning that it must be adjusted and appropriate to the conditions at any particular moment. Female newscasters are apparently taught to have a perpetual smile even when announcing the deaths of forty thousand people in an earthquake!

Maintaining the proper bearing will contribute to your effectiveness as a leader. Your manner is an outward manifestation of your inner self-confidence, and, like self-confidence, it is infectious as well. Subordinates simply expect their leaders to not only be confident and possess self-control but also to "look the part" and act accordingly.

Believing

The area of believing refers to the emotional abilities of a leader. They involve the leader's ability to inspire others and include the attributes of trust and respect, optimism, enthusiasm, humility, humor, and tact. An in-depth description of each quality follows.

It has always been true that leaders must earn the trust and respect of those whom they are leading. Although it is nice to be liked, it is far more important to be trusted and respected. Some individuals (e.g., Machiavelli) have subscribed to the notion that projecting an aura of fear is a key to leadership. Admittedly, this approach works sometimes and with some people. Unfortunately, however, individuals who respond to fear are often those who are least likely to contribute to the solution when an issue arises in which they have expertise.

One of the authors of this book served under eight university presidents during his career. "While each possessed many admirable qualities, I had different levels of trust and respect for each. My personal success was highly correlated with my perception of how much trust and respect existed between my president and me."

As Machiavelli observed, both fear and respect can be employed to achieve leadership success, and both must also be cultivated. Despite Machiavelli's argument to the contrary, the most desirable approach in today's society is leadership based on respect. Although effective temporarily, fear ultimately loses its potency, whereas respect grows and even multiplies.

It is helpful for a leader to have a realistic degree of optimism. Individuals usually choose to follow leaders who have a positive outlook and conveys to those being led that they can help them achieve common goals. The optimistic person sees the glass as half full, whereas the pessimist sees the glass as half empty.

One of the authors, who grew up on a small family farm, recalled that his father made essentially all of the family's decisions, and he was always optimistic. "He never started a crop that he didn't anticipate would produce a top yield. Likewise, I never submitted a research proposal I didn't expect to be funded." People want to follow leaders who believe in themselves and are confident and optimistic about achieving their goals.

A leader who is enthusiastic is more likely to get the members of the group and the organization to do their best. An enthusiastic individual who is passionate about the project at hand is better able to convince other members of the team that the objectives can be accomplished and that the project's challenges can be overcome. Hard work coupled with enthusiasm is a tried and true recipe for success.

The successful leader almost always displays a reasonable degree of enthusiasm. To others on the team or in the organization this attribute conveys that the leader believes in the effort.

Successful leaders recognize their imperfections but not to the point of allowing them to hamper their leadership. Admitting that one doesn't know the answer to a question does not detract from one's character. In fact, to demonstrate that one is human actually strengthens one's character. In the final analysis, humility simply shows that a person is human. Being humble also enables people to better appreciate those whom they are leading.

A healthy sense of humor can help keep a workplace upbeat and facilitate leadership. Successful leaders must take their work seriously but not take themselves too seriously. Having a sense of humor eases tension and helps make one's coworkers more relaxed and comfortable. It also sends the message that the leader is human and approachable. In being able to laugh at the things that are of little or no consequence, the leader gives permission to others to enjoy themselves and focus on the truly important aspects of the work.

However, humor can also become a serious handicap to leadership. Telling jokes and stories and trying to be the life of the party can easily backfire if not approached judiciously. Because too much comedy can detract from effectiveness, leaders should not become nominees for "comedian of the year." Indeed, many individuals have experienced career-ending situations because of their attempts at humor, particularly telling off-color jokes.

In agricultural circles, it is common knowledge that a once highly successful secretary of agriculture told an off-color, racist joke in a public setting. The result: his termination as secretary of agriculture. The old axiom "when in doubt—don't" is good advice.

Tact involves having a keen sense of what to do or say in order to maintain good relations with others and avoid offense. It is possessing sensitive emotional or aesthetic discernment. The individual who is tactful is empowered to make tough decisions and still leave others feeling good about themselves.

Character Attributes Are about Focus and Follow-Through

Character counts in all aspects of agricultural leadership, and the attributes associated with thinking, acting, and believing help one achieve and maintain good character. While not initially essential, the higher one advances, the more imperative it becomes that one acquire and develop as many attributes in the three highlighted areas as possible to keep the effort in balance. If it is not possible for one to acquire or develop the necessary attributes, one must find a way for the organization one leads to manifest them.

Successful leaders study the big picture and have the ability to analyze the entire situation and focus their efforts on accomplishing specific objectives. They understand that follow-through is necessary to ensure the goals are met and everyone is ready for the next step—whatever it might be.

Those who aspire to improve their leadership ability must become students of leadership. There is no better place to start a leadership course of study than with the cardinal virtues and the character attributes identified and explained in this chapter. Aspiring leaders should examine themselves carefully to ascertain where they excel and need improvement. It is also useful to evaluate other leaders or their own leaders with regard to how well they manifest the cardinal virtues. To what extent do they demonstrate the appropriate character attributes in the areas of thinking, acting, and believing? Becoming a more effective leader is a marathon, not a sprint, and it requires prolonged and persistent effort.

The truly successful leader possesses—in full measure—the cardinal virtues and a substantial portion of the character attributes in the areas of thinking, acting, and believing. There is little flexibility in not fully meeting the expectations of the cardinal virtues, as they are largely nonnegotiable. However, one can compensate for deficiencies in the latter category to some extent. For example, although humor is important, there are ways to overcome this shortcoming. There is no flexibility, however, in prudence; either you exercise it, or you do not.

In the final analysis, character counts, and it counts a great deal. To be a successful leader, an individual must become a student of leadership. This means always seeking ways to improve and hone one's leadership skills. While character describes and defines an individual, character can also be improved. Like character, leadership cannot be defined by a single event or situation. Rather, it is an accumulation of events and actions. It is a set of skills and capabilities that can be learned, strengthened, and improved. Leaders must continually assess their capabilities and identify and make changes in their leadership styles and approaches. This includes an ongoing assessment of one's character and subsequent improvement.

Tying together all of these dimensions is an effective approach in dealing with people, one that reflects a leader's positive attitude. The effectiveness of each essential virtue and many of the important virtues can be augmented by a leader's positive attitude, multiplying their impact and enhancing their value. This is easily demonstrated when observing a leader encouraging team members, praising them for their good work, *and* delivering positive comments on how a task might be improved if it failed to "hit the bull's eye" on the first try. Seeing workers at their work sites and not just in the leader's office is another way to build esprit de corps as well. Although not virtues per se, these actions are nonetheless essential since much of a leader's success depends on the positive attitude of those carrying out the program as well.

Case Studies

HOW LEADERSHIP CAN MAKE A DIFFERENCE

Frequently case studies provide examples of how others have addressed problems that may be similar to one that a reader is facing. Thus, case studies are used here to show leadership approaches in dealing with agricultural issues, especially those in research and outreach.

The format for the case studies is flexible, but each addresses the following points in some way.

1. What will this case study show? Each identifies the key leadership elements reflected in the case study.
2. Case study: It tells the "story," including situations that demonstrate leadership strengths and weaknesses. It contains enough detail to clearly explain the situation and show the leader's successes and failures.
3. Key leadership questions that are relevant: Because the readers are not in a discussion group, it is important that they recognize some of the leadership questions that are addressed in the case study.
4. Results: What happened in terms of results? Each case study presents at least the highlights so that the readers can see how the story ended and the problem areas that were identified and needed to be resolved.
5. Comments: The case study author's additional comments may broaden the readers' understanding of how the case study may be used when appropriate.

1. Facing Down Nature: How a Regional Lab Survived Hurricane Katrina

What Will This Case Study Show?

Key points include the following: (1) finding people after the storm; (2) housing them at temporary locations; (3) providing resources for personnel, supplies, and equipment; (4) communicating with personnel who were located across the country; (5) implementing a different form to handle those manifesting disciplinary problems; (6) returning home; (7) repair of the center; (8) continuing productivity after the storm; (9) assessing damage; and (10) coordinating the return of personnel to the center.

Case Study

The USDA's Southern Regional Research Center (SRRC), headquartered in New Orleans, Louisiana, is operated by the agency's Agricultural Research Service (ARS). Strongly committed to multidisciplinary commodity-use research, it houses chemists, entomologists, food technologists, plant pathologists, and several other scientific specialties under one roof.

The center continues to develop innovative uses for cotton and various agricultural products. Scientists based there are working to find solutions to dangerous crop-contaminating molds—mycotoxins—as well as invasive termites that cause $1 billion worth of damage each year in the United States. The SRRC researchers are also trying to make life easier for millions of people around the world who suffer from peanut allergies by searching for less allergenic peanut varieties.

LEAVING DESTRUCTION IN ITS WAKE

On August 29, 2005, the SRRC joined much of New Orleans and the Mississippi Gulf Coast in coping with Katrina, a powerful category 4 hurricane. The storm wreaked havoc on the facility, plowing through dozens of windows and shearing off parts of the roof of the chemical wing. Mature evergreens and magnolias on the forty-acre grounds surrounding the center were flattened, opening pathways for encroaching floodwaters.

The water came from Lake Pontchartrain, which inflicted the most costly damage, moving water up the drainage canals in the wrong direction and into the city. Major canals on both sides of the center (each about a mile away from the SRRC) broke in several places, flooding New Orleans and leaving 80 percent of its land under water, especially the lakefront area, where the SRRC is situated. The rising waters poured in so quickly—and persisted so long—that five employees at the New Orleans–based facility who had volunteered to stay throughout the storm had to be rescued by boat.

Figure 2. SRRC under water. The floodwaters stayed for nearly three weeks in a hot and humid environment and caused $50 million worth of damage to the center.

The SRRC's ground-floor level remained under water for three weeks, setting the stage for widespread, aggressive mold growth (see figure 2). Laboratories and equipment in those areas were ruined. Experiments were destroyed. With no electricity, biological materials such as bacteria and fungi–which require constant refrigeration— were also lost, along with termite collections and other live samples. In the immediate aftermath of the storm, the first task was to determine the condition of more than 350 scientists and staff who had been scattered across the southeastern region of the United States and beyond by the mandatory evacuation order received from the mayor's office prior to the Katrina landfall. A temporary headquarters for the SRRC was activated by August 31 at the headquarters for the Mid-South ARS area in Stoneville, Mississippi, three hundred miles north of New Orleans.

MOST WORRISOME PERIOD

Following the storm, the most problematic task for SRRC administrators was accounting for all employees. A coordinated effort by the center and ARS's Mid-South Area Office helped locate all missing personnel in a timely manner. Although attempts were made to reach scientists and staff through their emergency numbers, it was discovered that some people had used phone numbers of contacts in the Greater New Orleans Area and along the Gulf Coast and thus were of little help after the storm.

Some people went to relatives' homes in Georgia, Virginia, Texas, South Carolina, Arkansas, and even locations much farther away. Although most were found within a week, it took several weeks for a few stragglers to be located. It took more than a month to find one employee who claimed he did not know he was supposed to call in. Not only was the status of scientists and staff important, but efforts were also made to locate each family member who lived with them. Fortunately, no one was lost in the storm, flood, or movement to temporary evacuation sites.

The second task was to provide cost reimbursements and living expenses to the employees. The USDA and the ARS approved per diems for employees and any dependent recorded on the 2004 Federal Income Tax Form 1040. This major move by the ARS headquarters in Washington, DC, allowed immediate help for center personnel and their families.

Both FEMA and the American Red Cross also provided immediate funds to help cover some costs even before the per-diem checks arrived at the employees' banks. Also quite helpful was the fact that the National Finance Center, which itself is housed in New Orleans, had alternate work sites already set up before the hurricane at three other locations around the country, enabling it to continue to pay employees without interruption.

The third task was to find laboratories around the nation where scientists and staff could be housed and that would have adequate support facilities to allow research to continue. Dozens of scientists and their support staffs had to relocate—many with lab equipment in tow—to several worksites in twelve states. Efforts were made to match scientists with university collaborators or with colleagues at an ARS laboratory and at universities doing compatible research. Even industrial collaborators and other USDA facilities offered space and support. So by October/November, two to three months after the flood, the SRRC was back in business.

This situation created several challenges. So as not to lose time, the center director pushed for the preparation of manuscripts based on data already gathered but not yet published in scientific papers. Between September 1, 2005, and August 31, 2006, 450 SRRC staff members had their names on professional papers. Research publications typically amounted to three-quarters of a normal year's output.

In addition, most of the samples needed for laboratory research were found either on the higher floors at the SRRC or as duplicates in other institutions. Some samples could not be reclaimed, particularly those that were held in freezers or refrigerators at the SRRC since electric power was not available for several weeks until a large generator was brought to the center. It was March 2006 before normal electric current again became available.

FIGHTING CONTAMINATION

To obtain many of the scientific materials and laboratory books and to recover relatively undamaged laboratory and facility equipment, the next task was to remove from the damaged SRRC all contaminated materials that were not in closed containers. For example, the chemical storeroom, located on the ground floor, had shelves that floated in the six feet of water and spilled bottles of toxic chemicals. Unless these were removed, commercial clean-up companies could not begin removing the deep muck on the ground-level floors.

As soon as they were allowed in by FEMA and the National Guard in early October, the directors from the Mid-South Area and the SRRC toured the facility to access the damage. To do so required medical clearances, proper shots, and protective clothing for anyone authorized to enter the building. Control of access was stringent. It soon became clear what needed to be done in terms of safety before any volunteering scientists could enter the building in order to clean up major contamination, and this was done under close administrative supervision.

Subsequently, when the scientific staff needed certain equipment at their interim locations, similar procedures were used to obtain the movable items from the upper floors, which had not been damaged. Each item was carefully and thoroughly decontaminated by SRRC personnel before the equipment was wrapped and shipped to the location where it was needed.

Key personnel from the ARS headquarters toured the facilities to assess the damage. By November 2005, it was clear that the loss was substantial and that an estimated $50 million would be required to get things back into functional operation. The issue of abandoning the site or building a new one was quickly aborted, for it would send the wrong message about the USDA's commitment to the area. The question was where and how to obtain the funds. Through ARS and USDA support, Congress moved to provide $35 million. The ARS had already committed $13 million. In fact, its whole repair and maintenance budget for FY 2006 (effective October 1, 2005) was designated for the rapid recovery. The SRRC provided $2 million from its own budget, which brought the total to $50 million.

The resources were obtained, but it took coordinated effort at all levels of the USDA and the US Office of Management and Budget, as well as congressional support, to put everything together. Within the ARS and the Mid-South Area headquarters, nothing was higher on the appropriations request than the SRRC recovery. It was important scientifically because of the major research efforts that were in operation, including cotton, rice, food safety, and sugar cane research, along with the very visible Formosan subterranean termite project. Recovery was also critical as it underlined the words of President Bush's often repeated statement that the federal government was in New Orleans to stay.

MASSIVE COMMUNICATIONS EFFORT

How were communications maintained with the scientific staff members, who were located ultimately at twenty-two different locations?

a. Almost daily telecommunications among the director and the research leaders were initiated, and as the crisis lessened, these took place on a weekly basis.

b. Daily e-mails with updates on the situation were sent to all personnel.

c. All of the research leaders visited every laboratory and every person under their supervision.

d. The director made personal visits to most locations.

What was needed was not only a constant flow of information about the SRRC situation but also updated estimates on how long would it be before the scientists, the staff, and their families could return to the New Orleans area. Further, each person was allowed to return, at government expense, to the New Orleans area to assess personal losses in home, facilities, and furnishings and to obtain critical papers needed to address insurance issues.

The SRRC personnel were encouraged by a visit from the director, for they felt that information shared at such visits was very valuable. Any personnel problem could be brought up, although almost all of these were taken care of by the research leader and the director's administrative office. One scientist became a major disciplinary problem, which ultimately required a joint effort by leaders from the SRRC, the Mid-South Area, the ARS, and finally the USDA's Office of General Council to dismiss the scientist after a return to New Orleans.

As the crisis eased and New Orleans started its recovery, one of the major challenges was to plan and execute the return of scientific and administrative personnel to the SRRC. Recognizing that the homes of fifty-six staff members had either been destroyed or needed major repairs, FEMA, with urging from the SRRC, the USDA, the ARS in Washington, DC, and the Mid-South Area Office, decided to locate a trailer park on the SRRC campus to provide housing for these staff members and their families. During the winter of 2005–2006, FEMA agreed to put fifty trailers with electric power, water, and sewerage service on the campus (see figure 3). Named after the director, this impressive site was called "Jordanville."

With the rapid cleanup of the laboratories under way and the trailer park available as temporary housing, the scientific staff began returning in April 2006. Some members of the administrative staff whose homes were not significantly damaged by the flood had already moved back in the fall of 2005. Thus they could work on a daily basis to ensure that the cleanup work was carried out efficiently and as rapidly as possible.

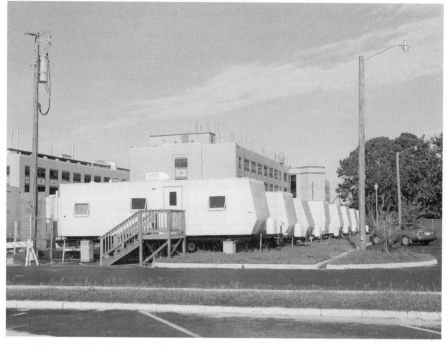

Figure 3. Fifty FEMA trailers served as temporary housing for scientists and staff while their homes were undergoing repairs. Some of the trailers were occupied for months.

MORALE BOOSTER

By July 2006, all personnel had been ordered back to New Orleans and SRRC. To accomplish all of this required considerable planning by the research leaders and the center's administrative officer. Travel orders, return of equipment that had been moved to scientists' temporary sites, and the ending of per diem had to be carried out. Because of major problems with mold, not all SRRC laboratories were ready by this time. With no central electric power for months, mold had grown up the walls from one floor to another and could be found even on the top floor. In some instances, significant portions of the walls had to be removed and replaced. The issue of mold-contamination effects on the human population and on scientific equipment was significant, and considerable time and effort were expended to remove this serious contaminant.

The massive return of staff was a morale booster for all the employees. They had been through a very difficult situation and survived it together. Their primary concern now was to finish the repairs and get back into full swing as quickly as possible. They also enjoyed seeing each other since many had been away from their SRRC colleagues for some time. They were also able to address the issues of repairing or selling their homes, and many of them picked up new homes that had not been damaged by the flood. The atmosphere at SRRC was exuberant!

Results

HIGHLIGHTS

The SRRC had technical staff planning and looking after the recovery by October 2005, within a month of the disaster. These recovery directors came from Washington, DC, and the Mid-South Area Office at Stoneville, Mississippi, and included SRRC staff and leadership as well.

The SRRC had most of its people back in New Orleans and on the SRRC campus beginning in April 2006; by July everyone had returned.

In addition, as mentioned earlier, 450 SRRC scientists were identified as authors on publications from September 1, 2005, through August 31, 2006. Production did not stop.

Most federal agencies in New Orleans averaged a net loss of 25 percent of their employees, individuals who left the organization or were permanently transferred because of the flood. The SRRC's gross loss was about 6 percent, but its net loss was 3.4 percent since some new personnel joined the SRRC after the hurricane and flood.

Good leadership was shown at most levels. It did not "come overnight" but had developed progressively during the years before Katrina. Personal attention to scientists and staff, including contract staff, paid off well. The keys to this were frequent communication to staff by leadership and the personal visits by research leaders and the director, all of which kept morale strong. This, it is believed, convinced almost everyone to stay with the center's program.

Undersecretary for Agricultural Research, Education, and Economics Gale Buchanan (who was also the USDA's chief scientist) visited the SRRC campus twice during the recovery, and Secretary of Agriculture Mike Johanns visited the campus in January 2007. Both came to witness the remarkable recovery, which was the result of a coordinated action plan that involved directors and staff members at all levels of the USDA and the ARS. Both individuals recognized the leadership that had been used to accomplish the recovery.

The situation at the SRRC was brought to the attention of the secretary and the undersecretaries of USDA. The matter was discussed at the secretary's weekly staff meeting, and everyone was kept abreast of the SRRC's progress. In 2007 the success of the concerted and major effort to reestablish the SRRC's research facilities and to procure the needed funds for the project was recognized with a special USDA Secretary Award.

PROBLEM AREAS THAT WERE IDENTIFIED AND
NEEDED TO BE RESOLVED:

The center's evacuation plan would normally have been effective, but the SRRC was not prepared for the flood that resulted from Katrina. Since then, key facilities are no longer at the lower level of the building. Now only offices for retirees, meeting rooms, and a lunchroom are on the ground level.

The emergency personnel tracking system did not meet the needs of this situation. Alternate phone numbers and addresses outside of the Gulf Coast area must be recorded for rapid access to personnel if another significant event should occur in the New Orleans area.

Further efforts have been carried out to ensure that all employees (permanent, temporary, student, or contract) know that they must call in to a prearranged telephone/computer within forty-eight hours of such an event.

Some Added Comments

The value of the trust that employees hold and treasure regarding their leadership should not be underestimated. Trust and commitment must be manifested from leader to employee and vice versa. When a crisis hits, that is when leaders are tested; it is then that the issue of control is really seen. Without it, there will not be a coordinated action plan, and people will seek ways to leave the organization.

Other leaders have said the same. Their words may differ, but as an example, Stephen Covey[1] expresses his thoughts in terms of a set of pillars such as "vision" and "discipline" (meaning focus and paying the price of leadership, respectively), along with "passion and conscience" (which relates to taking care of people). One of the authors remembers listening to Maj. Gen. William Dean of Korean War fame give a speech to ROTC cadets. Dean summarized leadership in three simple phrases: "know your job, take care of your people, and always tell the truth." All of these elements are seen in this case study.

Leadership Perspective

In terms of this work's leadership model, it is evident that the essential cardinal virtues of Prudence, Justice, Temperance, and Fortitude were important to the successful outcome of the event described.

Examples include the decision to get the organization operating again as quickly as possible (prudence), the authorizing of per diem to the center's employees in the aftermath of the disaster (justice), the efforts to contact all of the center's employees and account for them and their family members (temperance), and the willingness to carry out the clean-up process as expeditiously as possible (fortitude).

The "important" virtues were in evidence as well. Examples of thinking included the vision to see beyond the immediate disaster to the desired end state, along with decisiveness, flexibility, and creativity when addressing fiscal and operational issues. Acting included taking the initiative to get the employees back to work as soon as possible, along with the assertiveness and initiative it took to realize that objective, communication with the employees about their own status and that of the center, communication with the USDA, and the confidence and motivation provided by the director and his staff throughout the entire episode. Believing aspects included the reciprocal trust and respect between the employees and the directors, along with the optimism, enthusiasm, and humor associated with the establishment of "Jordanville," and the humility and tact involved in helping and convincing the employees to return and resume their productivity in support of the center's mission.

Although an extreme example, this case study illustrates an ideal level of support for the work's leadership model and superb corroboration of its validity.

2. Exerting Agriculture Leadership in Distributed Geographic Locations

Introduction

Like politics, most agricultural enterprises are ultimately local—site specific—depending on the surrounding ecosystem, proximity to markets, populations, and transportation, and a resulting evolution of farming and ranching practices.

While site-specific or at least regional research is often needed to support and promote these practices, general principles of agricultural science and technology can also be broadly applied. Accordingly, a combination of both site-specific and more general scientific activity has emerged in the university-based and federal systems that support food and agricultural enterprises in the United States.

In small states with relatively little geographic diversity, agricultural research is often centralized on the campuses of universities with few satellite sites in operation throughout the state. In larger states with more diversity, universities and federal agencies such as the USDA's Agricultural Research Service have developed various forms of geographically distributed but connected organizational structures that bring together the disciplinary variety necessary to meet the more heterogeneous needs of the regional industries. These structures also incidentally provided early opportunities for experience and leadership in multidisciplinary research using a systems approach.

For example, research on economics and research with regard to the use of natural resources can be both commodity specific at the local level and more generally applicable in regional, state, and national settings. Linking research and outreach (e.g., extension programs) with the more centralized basic and disciplinary research aimed at conceptual breakthroughs presents challenging, exciting leadership opportunities.

Texas A&M: A Large Distributed System

This case study deals with the evolution of one of the larger distributed systems of regional research programs and extension services as it evolved and operates today in the Texas A&M University System. Universities and federal agencies in many of the other large and ecologically diverse states developed similarly as distinct distributed models. All of them continue to evolve as needs, modern communications, and developments in science drive change.

In the Texas A&M example, there emerged a set of thirteen regional research and extension centers to support the state's ecologically varied agriculture. Shared leadership at multiple levels and with individuals from industry, government, and academia was required to develop a vision at the institutional level and to carry it to fruition at a number of locations across the state.

Shared ownership by university, state, and local participants was an important factor in the birth and sustained operation of these centers. Such joint leadership was also critically important in the operational phase—leadership in upper-level administration, in the campus-based academic departments, at the level of the regional centers, and with the government and industry players served by these centers. The creation of this collective vision and plan connected an effective, integrated, and dynamic set of networked research and extension activities that continue to serve Texas and the nation very well.

The major leadership elements portrayed in this case study are the following:

Visionary leadership that recognized the need and opportunities for a distributed but connected system of research and extension activities at various locations in a state

Shared leadership in the form of the joint setting of priorities and strategies between university administrators, local and state government officials, and private-sector stakeholders, which helped define the mission and secure the necessary resources

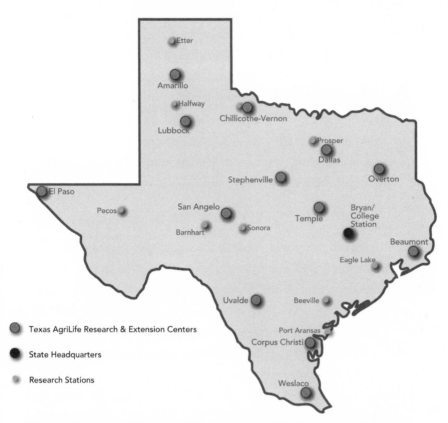

Figure 4. Location of Texas A&M University AgriLife Research and Extension Service centers.

Cooperation between university, federal, and private-sector elements in conducting regional research and extension programs

Leadership by administrators at the regional centers that
(1) brought together the multidisciplinary teams of research
scientists and extension specialists who addressed systems
research in support of regional agriculture and natural-
resource management; (2) maintained ongoing relationships
with regional stakeholders; and (3) fostered collaboration
between other regional centers and with campus-based
departments

Leadership by university-based department heads in bringing together the disciplinary activities of regional and campus-based
researchers into a complementary strategy—connecting basic
and applied research across the state

Graduate-student involvement in regional research, allowing for
joint mentorship by campus and center-based faculty—which
promoted active planning of academic and regional objectives
and was often the most effective linkage of all.

Genesis

The regional Texas A&M AgriLife Research and Extension Centers
(ARECs) (formerly known as Agricultural Research Extension Centers [ARECs]) evolved over a long period of time and along different
pathways. In some cases, initial "substations" evolved to become full-
fledged centers. In other cases, centers were new launches at critical
locations across the state. Earlier substations then became satellites
of the new centers or were closed. In some cases, the USDA ARS established similar commodity or site-specific locations. Often centers
were co-located with either ARS or the state agricultural experiment
stations (SAES) alternately being the host and the tenant. Leadership
in both of these institutions resulted in very closely knit complementary activities that still share resources and continue to be highly effective and efficient.

The architect of the modern ARECs at Texas A&M was Dean of
Agriculture Harry O. Kunkel, who was instrumental in bringing
together the state/regional leadership that established these Texas
centers, especially in the 1970s. Experiment Station Director Jarvis
Miller and Extension Service Director John Hutchison also were
closely involved in the genesis of these centers.

Neville Clarke, director of the Texas Agricultural Experiment Station in the 1980s, led the team that developed and implemented the
state and regional strategies that enabled the acquisition of new state
and federal resources for the centers. Planning with clear statements

of benefits and outcomes, legislative liaisons to secure new funding, and development of multidisciplinary research at several locations were key elements of the successes during this period. Also at this time, the ARECs gained major momentum in addressing both the opportunities and the challenges of the 1980s. Examples from this era follow.

Regional Research Leadership Examples

Resident directors of research provided leadership in the development of interdisciplinary research utilizing the systems approach in highly creative ways. For instance, Dr. Bill Holloway at the Uvalde AREC developed and his team implemented a very coherent strategy to optimize regional use of natural resources to generate income from both wildlife and commercial beef cattle ranches that had to operate as commercial entities. His team was supported by involved ranchers and scientists from the relevant academic departments at the main Texas A&M campus.

Beef cattle production often involves several stages, beginning with cow-calf operations, followed by maturing of weaned calves (stockers) grazing on winter pasture and final fattening in feedlots. These occur at different locations in Texas. As in the commercial beef-production system, calves from the Uvalde Center were moved to other ARECs involved in stocker forage research at several locations in the state, including the Angleton Station (Marvin Riewe, superintendent), the Overton AREC (Charles Long, resident director), and the El Reno ARS facility in Oklahoma (operated at the time by Floyd Horn, later administrator of the ARS). Cattle were moved later to feedlot research operations at the Amarillo AREC (David Hutchison, principal investigator). This allowed research on the same set of cattle spanning multiple regional stages of the production cycle. The overall experimental design allowed study of performance from birth to slaughter in statewide and highly diversified environments.

Another example of leadership for multidisciplinary research occurred at the Beaumont AREC, under the leadership of Resident Director Jim Stansel, where state and ARS scientists conduct a highly integrated rice research program. In the latter half of the 1980s, the rice industry in the Upper Gulf Coast region, represented by the Texas Rice Research Foundation (TRRF), recognized that it was losing its national and global competitiveness. It borrowed money to contribute to an expanded research and development effort to infuse the new technology to return to a sustainable level. New products from the rice-breeding program, along with the companion production system technology, allowed the industry to return to sustainable economic competitiveness.

Multidisciplinary teams of both campus and center-based scientists and extension specialists working together developed integrated cropping systems that combined enhanced germplasm, improved soil- and water-management practices, integrated pest management, and marketing strategies. The system has a measured rate of return on investment of research funds of more than 100 percent per year.

Examples of such systems are the short-season cotton-production system for the High Plains of Texas, disease-resistant sorghum-production systems for the Texas Coastal Bend, and integrated production systems for horticultural crops in the Rio Grande Valley.

The efficiency of water use in irrigated agriculture was markedly improved by the development of drought-tolerant crops and by increased water-use efficiency through the use of a low-energy, precision-agriculture (LEPA) watering system. The LEPA delivers water near the ground under low pressure, avoids evaporative losses, and reduces pumping cost. The Texas Water Resources Institute (TWRI) provided funding for and facilitated the adoption of the LEPA method at several locations in Texas.

In centrally planned research conducted at multiple locations across the state, both plant and animal geneticists collaborated in conducting trials on germplasm at the various centers to discover genotype × environment interactions and the extent to which technology is applicable to different environments and crop-production systems.

In each of these continuing efforts, organizing and maintaining the collaboration between and the active engagement of both campus-centered researchers and regional stakeholders have been keys to success. In more recent times, such integrated systems have emerged for the development of high-energy crops for biofuels.

Distributed Locations: Challenges and Opportunities

The AREC directors and faculty find themselves immersed in the communities they serve. The metaphor is that these individuals and their families live in the community fishbowl—meaning they are highly visible at all times. They clearly do not enjoy the anonymity the ivory tower affords their campus colleagues. This provides both major advantages in understanding the needs of clientele and gaining support from the users of their products. It also poses some risk of becoming overly immersed in immediate issues of the day, which can work to the detriment of the longer-term research objectives, which are the centers' primary mission. Leadership at the level of the AREC directors is very important in ensuring the proper symmetry between these two motivating factors—balancing immediate operational responsiveness and the need to create new knowledge that meets day-to-day requirements and crises, which are always present. Shared leadership by the campus-based department heads and resident directors as they mentor individual scientists within their disciplines also helps maintain this balance.

Senior administrators in the Texas A&M System created a procedure for research planning and staff-performance evaluation in regional centers. The system clearly enunciates a set of expectations and ensures parity between campus- and center-based faculty. Scientists in the centers are jointly evaluated by their disciplinary department

head and their regional director. Recognition is given to collaborative research. This has produced a "one-class" system of professionals
no matter where they are located. Academic titles are also used for
scientists in the regional centers.

With the advent of the biotechnology revolution, regional scientists have sometimes been challenged to develop and maintain a cutting-edge research capacity in the face of limited access to expensive
equipment. As the ARECs have evolved, they have had to become
more aggressive in securing funding from a variety of sources. They
have moved past the earlier support from mainly core state and federal funding sources to competitive grants from both government
and industry.

In the Texas A&M System, numerous regional scientists use very
sophisticated methods and equipment to meet the needs of regional
clientele. In this respect their work has national and international significance. Leadership to promote and nurture collaboration between
centers and campuses has been critical to the balanced evolution of
capacities and productivity in the ARECs.

Lessons Learned

The advent and operation of the ARECs in the Texas A&M AgriLife
programs depended on effective, shared visionary and operational
leadership at many organizational levels. It is an ongoing institutional
challenge to maintain the organized commitment to such leadership
as senior administrators in the university setting, leading state and
local government officials, farmers, ranchers, and industry personnel
come and go.

Interdisciplinary and interinstitutional relationships are fragile
and difficult to maintain. The regional stakeholders' expectations for
research are high. The level of support for the programs that generate
these products is also very high when programs are perceived to be
responsive to needs. Leadership in both industry and the university
must work effectively to ensure recognition for both campus and re-

gional research and extension faculty in providing these products. A continuing challenge is the acquisition of support from industry operators for longer-term investments in new technology as opposed to immediate problem solving.

Like other areas of agricultural research enterprise around the country, core resources for the ARECs have been seriously eroded by the combination of inflation and reduced funding. Although the ARECs are sometimes not as competitive for federal funds as academic departments, leadership at the regional level and the creativity of AREC faculty members have enabled the centers to effectively diversify their portfolios as a means of securing complementary resources from multiple sources.

Team research involving various disciplines and locations is generally challenged by a long-standing but possibly somewhat improved limitation in the academic recognition-and-reward system, which still favors single-author publications in peer-reviewed journals. While the major scientific and economic impact of research in the ARECs receives growing recognition at Texas A&M, the current recognition system can still be a problem.

A matrix management approach involving a combination of disciplinary and interdisciplinary leadership provides the scientific depth and the problem-solving breadth to meet the demands for agricultural science-and-technology products in a state whose agricultural environment is one of the nation's most diversified and supports more than sixty economically significant commodities. Shared leadership is vitally important to promoting, enabling, and rewarding performance that creates and maintains the "three Cs" of engagement— communication, cooperation, and collaboration.

Leadership Perspective

The success of the AREC project provides substantial support for the essential tenets espoused in this work's leadership model. The essential cardinal virtue of Justice was paramount in this case study, as the ARECs were essentially research collaborations working constantly to strike an appropriate balance between the rights and needs of self-interest and the rights and needs of others. Fortitude was quite evident as well, given that this system evolved over time and thus required endurance and perseverance to survive and succeed. Throughout the process, examples of Prudence and Temperance were manifest, as competing desires clashed that required thoughtful and reasoned consideration in situations that had no easy answers.

Evidence of the model's "important" virtues was apparent as well. Acting began by establishing and ensuring communication among the various centers, substations, and other organizations involved in the effort. These exchanges fueled the initiative to expand and enhance the program's capabilities, which motivated others to become involved and engendered confidence in those already participating. The integrity of the participants allowed for modest risk taking, which allowed for more ambitious practices to emerge, thereby increasing the program's overall effectiveness by improving its capabilities and results.

Believing aspects began with the tact with which organizers approached the consortium idea in this case study, tinged with humility in their belief that it was for the betterment of all and not simply for one station and/or a select group of individuals. Once entered into, trust and respect became the operating motives within the groups to ensure that all remained true to the effort's larger objectives, which inspired both optimism and enthusiasm in those working in ARECs and others observing their efforts in the "community fishbowls."

Thinking began with the efforts to develop and disseminate a vision involving cooperative efforts that would allow for the emergence of synergy within the Texas A&M Regional ARECs. Once established, creativity and flexibility surged to the fore, allowing for the program and the system to emerge as agents of change for these types of efforts in Texas and around the country.

In the limited-asset environments in which Agricultural Research and Extension Centers operate, conceiving and proposing shared-leadership endeavors are difficult enough; realizing them and having them flourish are altogether more unusual occurrences. This case study provides a remarkable example of how an idea of this type can succeed and provides substantial validation for the elements of the work's leadership model.

3. Closing and Relocating Facilities and Terminating Programs

Introduction

One of the most challenging aspects of leadership in the academic environment is keeping research programs relevant, ensuring adequate and appropriate facilities for research, and keeping all activities in line with available resources. While these challenges sound simple and straightforward, they are fraught with pitfalls that can spell disaster for administrators. Consequently, the successful leader can minimize the risk and ensure success if all aspects of such actions are clearly recognized, planned for, and executed in a proper way.

No Shortcuts

Effective leadership requires that closing or relocating a facility or terminating a program be taken with minimum negative impact on continuing programs. It is much easier to initiate the building of a new facility or the founding of a new program than to kill a program or close, relocate, or reassign a facility. Although these are exceedingly challenging tasks, there are ways to improve the opportunity for success—or at least minimize the costs or negative impact on the leader or on existing programs.

The leader who must make adjustments in programs (e.g. close, relocate, or reassign a facility or terminate a research program) must first realize there are no shortcuts. Taking the action is quite easy if the leader has the necessary authority, but the real task is to take the action while leaving everyone concerned feeling that they have won.

Logical Steps to Success

Leaders must take a series of logical steps to ensure success. The examples in the upcoming case studies will show the following:

1. The need for closing, relocating, or reassigning facilities and terminating research programs is universal, especially in dynamic research efforts or during austere budget climates.
2. Planning and doing one's "homework" in any situation is important in reaching a satisfactory conclusion.
3. The process of taking action can be accomplished with a minimum of negative problems if, after doing one's homework, one follows a series of logical steps and stays with the plan.
4. A staff can be exceedingly helpful in focusing on the preliminary assessment of a proposed action. However, the leader should personally assess the pros and cons requiring any major action. This step is critically important. First, get all the information possible—from both those who agree with your proposal and those who will likely oppose your idea.
5. The naysayers' opinions and ideas are important because these people can enable you to sharpen your message in order to build general support for your proposed action. It is very likely that some of your personal staff will have different ideas and opinions, especially if your style of leadership fosters openness. The astute leader quickly recognizes that staff can be helpful. Of course, when a decision is finally made, the naysayer on staff must be on board as the process moves forward and must support the leader's decision.

To take a drastic action once the leader is convinced of the necessity of doing so, the leader should start with the entire staff. These are the people nearest to the leader and who can and should be the leader's greatest assets in such an undertaking. These people can not only ask the toughest questions but, more important, can also help the leader respond to the toughest questions that others ask.

The successful leader encourages open discussion on important issues until everyone has had an opportunity to express any concerns or state their support or lack thereof. This generally occurs until a leader reaches a decision. Then the entire staff should be on board.

The leader must know the staff members are committed. It is not enough for them to just agree with the boss. It is important for the staff to be wholeheartedly supportive and willing to help sell the idea. Recognizing the need for taking such actions is important. If the leader does not have confidence in this step, the idea should be put on the back burner for review or for later consideration. Of course, at some point, the staff should understand that, after a decision is made, the proposed action articulated by the leader must be supported even if a staffer is not completely sure that it is the best answer. When the leader is comfortable with this step and all staff members are working together, then the next step can begin. When a pebble is thrown into a lake, the ripples move in ever larger concentric circles. This type action is sold in similar fashion. After the leader has made a decision, the process can move to the next "concentric ring."

First, start with those individuals who would be most affected by the proposed action. This group will probably be the most difficult to sell because they have the most to lose. Those who have the most to gain oftentimes are comfortable where they are and see no need to risk change. Always keep in mind that surprises should be kept to a minimum. Avoiding surprises enables you to keep control of the situation.

Always Consider Personnel

The astute leader realizes that any action involving terminating a program or closing or relocating a facility quickly boils down to personnel. As part of the homework, the leader thinks ahead and establishes ways in which actions can affect personnel. Here are some sound guiding rules. Carefully seek ways to minimize negative impact on personnel. Identify options for them.

1. Always be honest and above board.
   - Do not be overly positive or negative.
   - Be careful of every word because your words ultimately become "written in stone."
2. Do not promise too much or too little.
3. Give a time frame for all proposed actions.
4. Always put your commitments in writing and make sure they are communicated to those who are affected. Never, never make a commitment that cannot be honored.

Once all organizational personnel are advised and are on board, it's time to move toward the next concentric ring. This involves individuals who are not directly affected by such actions (e.g., farmers, agribusiness personnel, elected officials, and people in related industries) but may have a vital interest in them.

Obviously, individuals and organizations who are your best supporters should be addressed quickly. Of course, in the early contact group are those who are affected the most. For example, if a cattle-research facility is to be closed, then the cattle industry should receive first attention. Making such contact should be personal, usually face-to-face meetings. It's appropriate to bring others who can contribute to selling the idea, but this is a time when the leader must be present.

It would be wise to work most closely with the leaders or "early adopters" among the clientele. The two key questions often asked by supporters such as commodity, trade, and special-interest groups are (1) what is the purpose of the action, and (2) how will the interest of our group be addressed after the action? Good leaders will have done their homework and be able to easily respond to these questions.

Each of the groups mentioned up to this point can be dealt with on an intellectual level. Sound, well-thought-out arguments will usually carry the day. For example, explanations can be given for the lack of adequate resources; other, perhaps more innovative, ways of tackling the problem can be presented; and the requirements for the project can be changed. Such clarifications and alternatives may convince these groups. Unfortunately, the leader must also deal with another group that does not address the issue on an intellectual basis. Some issues must be dealt with politically, and reasonable arguments simply are not considered. Here are a few examples:

Example #1: Faculty and Staff Reassignments

In a tight budget situation, a soybean extension specialist position was lost. There simply were not sufficient resources to continue funding the position. The involved department head developed a plan that recommended to the director that he redirect the assignment of one of two peanut specialists since both soybeans and peanuts are oilseed crops.

On the surface, this appeared to be a very logical approach, particularly during tough budget times. The college dean and the director very quickly did an assessment and, with the department heads, agreed with the solution. Support from key commodity groups and leading farmers was sought and granted. This was not unexpected because many peanut farmers are also soybean farmers. The action was announced late one afternoon.

Early the next morning the dean received an urgent phone call from a very powerful legislator who inquired, "What the hell are you doing?" By his tone the message was clear. The dean responded that he and the extension service director would be in the legislator's office before the end of the day. As soon as they arrived and started to explain about the budget, the legislator quickly said, "I know your budget situation. In fact, we are going to be working on your budget later this week." With a knowing twinkle in his eye, he asked the dean and the director whether they could find another way to cover the soybean position. Not being completely stupid, the dean and the director quickly assured the legislator that they could. Later that day they countermanded the action from the day before. This was not a satisfying intellectual experience, but it was certainly a great lesson in the perils of leadership. There are politicians who control funding who are not necessarily driven by logic or intellectual approaches. They have other tactics and agendas, and those sometimes carry greater weight. In this particular case, one of this legislator's key political supporters was a peanut farmer who did not grow soybeans, and the farmer feared diminished support for peanuts. This also shows how critical it is for leaders to check all bases before announcing a change.

Example #2: Closing Research and Extension Facilities

In view of budget constraints, an experiment station director decided to close a departmental research farm. After doing all of the necessary in-house due diligence with university, trade, and commodity groups, the dean secured appointments with the chairs of the House and Senate agricultural committees in the state legislature. After listening to the well-defined plan, the chairs said they would handle the politics. They thanked the director, and the closure went off like clockwork.

Example #3: Moving and Consolidating Programs

Another great learning experience involved moving and consolidating programs. Budget problems are never pleasant, but they sometimes give administrators opportunities to address problems nearly impossible to solve in good budget times.

An extension service staff member recommended consolidating two extension locations, something that had been discussed for a number of years. However, political sensitivity about the move precluded taking action until a tight budget created an opportunity. The dean already knew that both the personnel involved and the host institution, which needed the space for other programs, supported the consolidation. There were only political concerns, such as a nod from both a gaining legislator and a losing legislator regarding jobs and personnel in their districts. Of course, the gaining legislator was in favor of consolidation.

The proposed action was discussed at a meeting involving the administration, the two legislators, and a few other key people. The losing legislator had been in a powerful position but had lost much of his power when the House "flipped" in terms of the majority party. Even though the argument to persuade him was a strong one, he did not like the idea at all and said no in a very forthright way: "Dean, if I was [sic] in my previous job, I'd ensure your budget was cut by exactly the amount of dollars you are removing from my district," he said. Nevertheless, knowing the legislator was not in his former powerful job and that he was unlikely to get it back, the dean went forward with the consolidation the next day.

These examples reflect distinctly different outcomes with varying degrees of success. In the case of consolidating the soybean/peanut position, some faculty and lower-ranking administrators were quoted as saying, "The dean wimped out." They might be correct. In the case of consolidating the extension service locations, it was a calculated risk with the odds in favor of the dean.

Example #4: Saying "No" to New Programs

Although terminating a research program is quite a challenge, starting a program can also have pitfalls for an administrator. Among them is that experiment station administrators can sometimes get into political situations that are not based on good science. One experiment station director found himself in political conflict over the science behind petiole testing for nitrogen fertility in cotton. A neighboring state was making extravagant claims, based on petiole testing, of increased cotton yields from additional nitrogen. This caught the attention of cotton farmers in the director's state.

Working through the state cotton organization, cotton farmers came to see the director to learn why his station was not "interested" in helping his state's cotton farmers. They appealed to the director's commitment to the state's agricultural industry. They had also been one of the station's best political supporters. The director was also generally knowledgeable about the particular testing program. He was not impressed by the claims and tried to convey that he did not see them as relevant for their state.

"Why can't you do some research to convince us of what you are saying?" was their comeback. Very reluctantly, the director agreed to do that, especially in light of a grant they provided to support the research.

So far no problem. However, the director was aware that the soil scientist who was the most appropriate person to do such research was a very distinguished, highly qualified, and somewhat cantankerous scientist. The scientist and the director had been colleagues before the director moved to administration, so the director was aware that the title of "experiment station director" carried zero influence with the scientist. Without mincing words, the eminent scientist declined the offer. "Even you should be smart enough to read the literature and see what a waste it would be to do research on this topic," he said.

The director pointed out the success being reported in the neighboring state. The scientist was disdainful of this neighboring state's scientists' research and was irritated that the director was asking him to do what he considered "useless research." However, a few hours later the scientist called the director and said he understood the latter's dilemma and the need for good relations with the cotton industry. In light of that, he would do some research—not for intellectual reasons but for the director on a personal basis.

At the end of the year, his research proved him correct: the neighboring state's scientists had quietly abandoned their recommendation for petiole testing for nitrogen because they had been thoroughly discredited.

Example #5: Acquiring New Land
Purchasing land is often challenging in the academic environment. While serving in an administrative position, an experiment station

director learned that there was a need to decrease the amount of rented land by purchasing comparable land for research that would be under the total control of the experiment station.

The three most important steps in making land purchases are as follows: (1) exhaustive analyses to establish need, (2) location of appropriate and acceptable land, and (3) funding in hand to make such a purchase.

In this example, steps 1, 2, and 3 were accomplished in fine fashion. Step 1 was easily accomplished and supported by faculty and the related industry. Step 2 was clinched when a suitable tract of land became available that was already surrounded on two sides by experiment station land. The previous owner had been a commercial seed company that had left the property in fine condition for research.

In Step 3, funds had been acquired from faculty grants and the sale of station timber. Funds were "in the bank."

Thus, it appeared to this director, the purchase of the land was a slam dunk. An appropriate request was sent through university channels to the governing board (a board of regents). While this was done in the winter months, plans were already under way as to how to use the new land as the spring planting season approached.

However, notice was quickly received that the request to purchase the land was rejected because the asking price was too high. One regent indicated to the board's "bean counters" that good farm land could be purchased for at least $200/acre less than the price the experiment station recommended. This did not appear to be a problem, though, because the director felt that the extra $200/acre could be easily justified. The director's staff also agreed that good farmland out in the county away from the station headquarters would sell for at least $200/acre less than would this particular tract, which was adjacent to the station and also near the city limits.

The director also provided detailed, documented information that the extra cost could be justified in less than two years by decreasing travel time and expenses on the part of scientists engaged in conducting research. In fact, it would probably take only one year to cover the extra cost of the land in savings by the experiment station. This appeared to be iron-clad justification for going $200/acre above the "going price" of land farther out in the county. The dissenting regent, however, was unmoved by such definitive data and continued to block the purchase. The stalemate lasted for more than a year, with repeated inquiries and provision of additional justification.

After almost giving up, one day one of the director's department heads indicated that one of his faculty was a good buddy of the regent. He said that if the director gave him the "go ahead," he would see what he could do. The director told him to proceed but never discussed the matter with the faculty member. All the director knew is that the next time this request came before the board, the regent, while not voting favorably for the purchase, did not block it. The new land became an integral part of the experiment station's research assets.

Another Example: Dealing with Legacies

On the first day of work, a newly appointed dean of a college was given a tour of a new animal science facility. Construction was about 80 percent complete. Within a few days, the dean received a call from the provost, who inquired about the status of the building. It was quickly obvious that the provost knew far more about the animal science facility than the dean did. He listened to the results of the dean's first visit and ventured new information.

"We want the livestock show arena, which was a part of the facility, moved to another location off the main campus," the provost said. He argued that the arena no longer fit the original location as an integral part of the animal science complex because of other new structures on campus. He also indicated there was a problem with one regent. The dean assured him he would do what he could.

Because he was new, the dean was cautious about making promises or speaking before learning the "lay of the land." While desiring to please his new boss, the dean certainly wanted to confer with his department of animal science before making any commitments. He started with his own staff. They were solidly in support of moving the livestock show arena to a more distant location, preferably to the animal science farm. The dean then met with the department head and faculty leaders, then with all faculty. He got 100 percent support from the departmental administration and the rather diverse faculty. Everyone agreed that, with recent developments on campus, the original plan was out of date. The livestock show arena should be relocated to a site off the main campus.

The dean then talked to some clientele commodity groups and found there was not much interest in locating the arena where it was originally planned (on the main campus). Armed with essentially unanimous support for relocating the arena, the director of university governmental affairs and the dean scheduled a meeting with the "questioning" regent.

After arriving at the regent's office, pleasantries were exchanged. The regent made it clear he did not care how much information was provided and that the arena would be built where it was originally planned and approved by the board as an integral part of the animal science complex. He said it was not his problem the university had built all the new buildings "in the way" of the animal science complex. This looked like a dead end until the dean learned a few weeks later that the governor would not reappoint the regent to the board of regents.

Consequently, the dean quickly sent a letter to the provost recommending the university request a change order to the board of regents to relocate the arena. Subsequently, the arena was relocated.

However, that's not quite the end of the story. The university governmental affairs officer and the dean believed that the honorable thing to do was to attempt to make peace with the regent—now that he was no longer on the board. They scheduled a visit. Peace was not to be, unfortunately. First, the dean and the governmental affairs officer were kept waiting in the regent's outer office for a long time. After brief pleasantries, the regent got right to business.

"I don't like what you have done," he said, looking at the dean and warning, "If I go back on the board, you'll pay." As it turned out, he did not get another appointment to the board, and so the dean escaped his payback.

These examples illustrate that closing or relocating facilities and terminating or initiating programs require doing one's homework, but, even then, success isn't always ensured. The examples point out that facts and logic often prevail. This is not necessarily the case in the political realm. With the politically appointed regent and the state legislator, logic and facts counted for little.

In the case of the regent, he was unhappy the university had taken land that had long been a part of the agricultural campus for other uses and just wanted to keep some cows in clear sight of the rest of the university's colleges and schools.

In the situation that involved the two peanut specialists and the lack of a soybean specialist, the legislator was responding to a local peanut (and not soybean) farmer. This particular peanut farmer was one of the legislator's big political supporters.

In the situation in which a legislator opposed the closure of a facility in his district, he just did not want to lose jobs in his district.

These situations provide lessons that are useful in many situations. First, unfortunately, it is not uncommon that power trumps logic and facts. It is important for leaders to do their homework and get as many people in their organization behind them as possible. They should never lose because they failed to do the homework. Additionally, although it is important to minimize risk, at some point one must take a certain degree of risk. Also, leaders should always hope for a little luck (as with the regent rotating off the regents board) and take advantage of such situations when they occur. Another very important lesson is that, when you see you are in a no-win, dead-end situation, it is best to extricate yourself immediately. Do not ever just hope things will work out. Unfortunately, often things fester and get worse. If you have to "eat crow," do it in one big gulp!

Results

In each of the instances cited, a favorable outcome was achieved. When a leader has made a decision on closing or relocating a facility or terminating a program, then every effort should be made to carry it out. The question remains, however, how can damage be minimized and success achieved?

Leadership Perspective

This chapter illustrates, in terms of the work's leadership model, that even though others may fail to adhere to the essential cardinal virtues of Prudence, Justice, Temperance, and Fortitude, it remains important for leaders to practice them in order to maintain their own integrity and credibility. In fact, in the face of unscrupulous dealings that are lacking in the areas of prudence and justice (e.g., instances of undue political influence and/or personal vendettas), the virtues of temperance and fortitude become all the more important in achieving outcomes that are both beneficial and honorable (e.g., reducing programs or facilities that are no longer productive, making the best use of taxpayers' dollars).

The value of the companion "important" virtues is evident as well. Examples of thinking included the ability to remain focused on the goal when faced with competing factors beyond one's scope of influence and the flexibility and creativity to develop methods of achieving the desired objective in such situations. Acting required maintaining the confidence of one's convictions, preserving one's integrity and bearing while in the thick of the action, a willingness to take a certain amount of risk when warranted, communicating with all who are (or may be) involved in a particular situation or issue, and being assertive while taking the initiative necessary to see the efforts through to a successful conclusion. Believing aspects included doing all that is required to maintain the trust and respect of key constituents, expressing a requisite level of optimism, enthusiasm, and humor when faced with adversity, and exhibiting humility and tact while working to persuade others to support your initiatives.

While not every situation in the chapter resulted in a resounding victory for the leaders involved, the situations nevertheless provide excellent examples of how leaders can and should act with honor in the pursuit of their objectives and of the fact that how one arrives at a particular outcome may be just as important as the outcome itself, especially since leaders and organizations' reputations often outlast the time or influence of unscrupulous individuals.

4. National Research Initiative:
Creating a Shared Leadership Vision

Introduction

The US Department of Agriculture's Agricultural and Food Research Initiative (AFRI), which began in 2009, is part of the new National Institute for Food and Agriculture (NIFA) but had its inception and early advocacy in the 1980s and early 1990s. It was called the National Research Initiative (NRI).

With a modest beginning of only $73 million, the NRI has been sustained over the ensuing years and is now enjoying a renaissance with new structure and increased funding. From 1991 through 2008, the NRI has provided about $2.3 billion for research. It has provided a focused resource for research in the sciences basic to food, agriculture, and natural resources and has supported new starts over a relatively broad spectrum of research.

The NRI is included as a case study because it represents an unusual event in the evolution of agricultural sciences that occurred in the midst of the so-called biotechnology revolution and because leadership was a critically important ingredient in this evolution. Leadership was necessary in the following phases:

Providing a vision
Gathering consensus—university, industry, government
Developing an action plan
Marketing the concept
Implementing the plan
Ultimately securing funding and setting up the infrastructure for
    the program
Sustaining and enhancing the program, once initiated

Leadership was shared—its players changed over time. The visionaries were, in some cases, replaced by advocates and implementers, but a few were involved throughout the process. Leadership was manifested in multiple ways. Most of the elements of leadership defined in this book were involved in one form or another in the evolution of the NRI. A number of leaders were involved in *making* it happen. Others were important players in *allowing* it to happen.

Genesis

Generally, federal agencies that support a broad scientific research agenda defer to the USDA to support such research for agriculture, the funding for which has traditionally been small relative to its size and importance. At the onset of the biotechnology revolution, not only was funding for the new sciences not coming to agriculture, but the traditional sources of funding for the land-grant universities, the so-called formula funds, were rapidly eroded by conflicts in policy and by inflation.

The idea of a focused effort to secure visibility and support for the opportunities afforded by biotechnology arose from multiple sources but quickly coalesced around the development of the NRI. The ensuing broad-based consensus and united support for the NRI in the government, industry, and academia were seminal events that involved leadership in each of these communities.

Vision to Practice: Leadership at Multiple Levels

The National Academy of Sciences Board on Agriculture developed the major case statement for the NRI in 1989 under the leadership of Dr. Ted Hullar, its chair (followed by two updates in 1994 and 2000). The initial report called for a bold collective effort to support a competitive grants program to launch and sustain the initiative. Dr. Charles Hess, the incoming assistant secretary of agriculture for science and education, provided major leadership for the initiative, shepherding it through the budget-development process with the USDA and securing the support of Secretary of Agriculture Clayton Yeuter. Hess was a central figure in defining the vision for the initiative and was its most visible advocate in government and academia.

Dr. Frank Press, president of the National Academy of Sciences, broke with tradition and allowed a summary of the results of the Board on Agriculture report to be released in time for the proposal for the initiative to move from USDA to the president's Office of Management and Budget (OMB). Once at OMB, Dave Gibbons, the examiner for this sector of USDA, recognized the merits of the proposal nationwide. While the initial goal of $500 million was not achieved, a substantial item in the president's budget proposal for 1991 emerged and went to the Congress for disposition. Fortunately, there were several members of the OMB staff who valued the proposal nationwide. They recognized that the National Science Foundation (NSF) and the National Institutes of Health (NIH) were riding the crest of the science wave. Yet the critical nature of agricultural research in academia, in the Agriculture Research Service (ARS), and in industry very much needed a similar boost.

Building Broad Consensus

A critical factor in the success of the NRI was the sustained leadership of key visionaries and advocates for the initiative. In addition to Hess, Dr. John P. Jordan, then administrator of the USDA Cooperative State Research Service (CSRS) brought vision and strong leadership to the initiative, both at the outset and in subsequent years through his involvement inside and outside the government.

Hess and Jordan dialoged with lawmakers about the need for the program, usually on a one-to-one basis. They demonstrated a passion for the initiative as a way to keep American agricultural research as the major resource of its kind in the world. They were also supported by other federal agencies like the National Science Foundation. Within the USDA, the ARS saw an opportunity not only to support the initiative but also to benefit from it unless it siphoned off resources already basic to the ARS.

Dr. Neville Clarke, then director of the Texas Agricultural Experiment Station, took a one-year sabbatical and participated actively in the definition of the initiative and its advocacy with numerous stakeholders, including key leaders of the National Association of State Universities and Land-Grant Colleges (NASULGC), the professional and scientific societies related to agriculture, and the elected leadership of a broad array of commodity and farm organizations.

By then, the CSRS had initiated the first elements of a competitive grants program, and the scientific staff had provided invaluable support by informing stakeholders about the vision for the initiative and the opportunities it would provide. This broad base of stakeholders actively participated in the definition of the NRI, and with their resulting ownership, they became active advocates for the initiative with Congress and other branches of government.

Building Strength through Expanded Leadership

The proposal was presented to the leadership of the NASULGC Board on Agriculture, the related State Experiment Station, and the extension and higher-education committees on policy. These leaders, along with the president of NASULGC, were instrumental in obtaining broad support for the state-level organizations they represented. The chief executive officers of many land-grant universities lent their moral and financial support to the advocacy of the NRI. This made possible the strong and fully integrated recommendation of NASULGC to the Congress and the administration for support of the NRI. This included strong advocacy by the individual land-grant university leaders in gathering support from their individual state congressional delegations when advocating with the appropriations committees.

Congressional support for the NRI varied among members and committee leaders. The NRI arrived at a time when new funds could be added to the appropriations—as opposed to the current "net sums" game, where new starts required finding funds to offset the cost. Key committee leadership did, in fact, see the merits of the initiative and provided new start-up funds that served as a base for modest growth in the future. Private funds provided by the land-grant universities allowed the employment of professional advocates for the initiative, and this was important to the effectiveness of the campaign.

In subsequent years, the administration proposed increases in the NRI; to some extent, congressional leadership used some of the funds in this proposal for congressionally directed projects, which obviously limited the growth of the initiative but tended more often to use the special grants or directed research for the ARS instead of earmarking them for the NRI.

Even with strong support there were, however, negative voices who opposed the NRI from the beginning, including some members of the research community. For example, a few experiment station directors were not supportive, especially if their scientists were not accustomed to the competitive-grant approach. One even attempted to use congressional contacts to block the initiative from fear that future funds for the NRI would come from the formula funding base. Some in the ARS viewed NRI as a competitor and feared that the ARS base funding might be tapped to fund the initiative. Some cheered an OMB analyst's assessment that the chance of success for the initiative was like a "snowball in hell." Of course, none of the scenarios on which the fears were based ever happened. Even a few commodity groups were not certain about the approach and were skeptical of the NRI, but most were supportive.

Initiative's Brief History

During the eighteen-year life of the NRI there were various ups and downs, especially in 1996 and 1997. New resources were added in 1999, but another dip occurred in 2001. From time to time, congressional members tried to specify what needed to be addressed, much as they had become accustomed to doing with the special grants program. Significant increases were seen for NRI from 2003 through the final NRI year of 2008. However, these later increases, although major boosts, broadened the use of NRI funds to include extension and instructional efforts. For the ARS, the percentage of proposals its scientists prepared almost matched the percentage of dollars and successful proposals that were awarded.

Another key factor that helped to increase the funds available to NRI was that the chief scientist was almost always a member of the National Academy of Science. Together, the administrator of the agency in which the NRI was located and the chief scientist gave personal reports to members of the agriculture-related committees of the US House and Senate and also to those members on the appropriate subcommittees. Further, the chief scientists tended to occupy the position for two to three years. Thus there was a consistency of reporting mechanisms and subsequent accountability. The chief scientist could be drawn from the universities, the ARS, or even industry, which ensured continued base support.

Nonetheless, there were almost always efforts by congressional members to put more restrictions on the program, and some even tried to move money to the congressionally preferred, directed, special grants program. Steady hands were needed to prevent "robbing Peter to pay Paul." With the advent of the successor to the NRI, namely, the Agricultural and Food Research Initiative in 2009, the recognition of the place of competitive grants and formula or base funding shows that each has its place in agricultural research.

Lessons Learned

Some people believe there is a time and a place for new things—and that putting good ideas into practice is much easier if they fit into the appropriate part of the space-time continuum. Others believe that effective leadership can create the space and time for things to happen. Still others believe that the alignment of leadership at specific points in the space-time continuum has a random component—people arrived on the scene for different reasons but recognized an opportunity and came together to make a mark. For the NRI, it seems that some of all of these ingredients were at play.

Certainly the breakthroughs brought about by the biotechnology revolution created an opportunity for change. A competitive grants approach in the USDA was already emerging as at least one way forward for research, extension, and education with regard to food, agriculture, and natural resources. While not all universities benefited equally from the initiative because of differences in capacities, the competitive grants approach, which was well validated in other parts of the scientific community, was broadly accepted as having major merit for agriculture.

With the growing momentum in biotechnology, the shared leadership that emerged at the right time and place was able to enunciate and effectively advocate the approach that became the NRI. Moreover, the early and continuing progress and results confirmed and continued to support the program in the ensuing years. All of these components set the NRI in motion and sustained it over time. History suggests that the many leaders involved in the evolution of the NRI were critically important. The broad consensus that was built among an amazing diversity of individuals and the resulting consistent message to decision makers about the merits of the initiative, along with effective inspired communication, persuasion, and perseverance, made the case for the NRI compelling.

Leadership Perspective
Using the work's leadership model as a framework for analysis, the NRI case study provides support for our contention that leaders should conduct themselves in accordance with the leadership model's essential cardinal virtues of Prudence, Justice, Temperance, and Fortitude. Prudence was at the heart of this experience, as the very essence of the NRI initiative was one of introducing prudential judgment—in

the form of a competitive grant system to help select the most beneficial projects—into the research-funding process. Using careful selection methods as a guide, the resulting decisions about which projects
to fund and the proper discernment between the rights and needs
of self-interest versus those of the broader agricultural community
were largely just and true. This process, which helped leaders make
the best use of the available limited funds in order to do what best
satisfied all of their obligations, allowed those making the decisions
to distinguish among competing demands and make good decisions,
especially in situations involving large budgets, shared leadership,
and congressional oversight. Maintaining the integrity of the process
and perpetuating its existence required continued temperance—the
ability to practice restraint, self-discipline, and self-control and to
prioritize one's responsibilities over one's desires—and the ability
to remain focused on the objective of increasing available research
funding for agriculture and natural resources as a whole, as opposed
to the instinct to turn inward and protect one's existing assets. This
helped administrators and leaders recognize and accept the limitations of acceptable action over the course of NRI's development and
provided guidance for choosing among available alternatives at critical points along the way, especially during the challenging period of
1996–1997. The element of fortitude, which encompasses the traits
of forbearance, endurance, perseverance, and the ability and willingness to confront uncertainty, was also essential, as it helped propo-
nents remain resilient in the face of vacillating support and funding
over an extended period of time. Furthermore, the realization of this
initiative allowed them to demonstrate "character in action" as they
remained steadfast in their support and worked to discredit the program's critics and dissuade the naysayers. These essential elements
derived their formidable value from the program's strong grounding
in noble ideals that fell right in line with the model's essential virtues.

Once established, the "important" virtues helped enhance and extend
the program's effectiveness. Virtues associated with thinking included

the vision to develop a system to benefit the common good, agents of change committed to the idea and possessing the flexibility and creativity to gather support and gain consensus, and the decisiveness to bring the efforts to fruition. These change agents were acting by communicating with one another and their key constituents. They buoyed up each others' confidence and motivated others to embrace their cause while taking the initiative to create and maintain a solid and influential coalition that was assertive enough to be effective, get the program funded, and ensure its continuation. Believing aspects were illustrated by the enthusiasm with which they approached their task, the optimism they managed to generate and sustain among key legislators, the trust and respect which accompanied the promised and realized results of the proposals, and the consistent tact with which the group went about conducting its negotiations and achieving its objectives.

In the case of the NRI, virtue was indeed its own reward. Honorable conduct that manifested character was evident throughout, which resulted in the realization of a program and an approach that were both efficient and effective—a rare victory with respect to congressional endeavors.

5. Battling Formosan Subterranean Termites

What Will This Case Study Show?

This case study demonstrates challenges relating to organizing research and outreach programs among institutions over which one has no direct authority. It also uses modern science to address both a half-century-old problem and unanticipated problems that cropped up during the implementation of a complex program.

Case Study

A CONGRESSIONAL VISIT (1997)

What a beautiful day it was, and how exciting it was likely to be! The congressman in whose district the Southern Regional Research Center (SRRC) is located was coming to visit the center. Rep. Bob

Figure 5. An example of the damage done to a dwelling by Formosan subterranean termites in a relatively short period of time.

Livingston arrived on time with staff, including his district representative, Rick Legendre. They arrived full of enthusiasm—just the kind
of attitude the center staff had hoped to see.

They toured the center, reviewed parts of every program, and did
it all quickly in one and a half hours. To say Livingston was pleased
is really an understatement. Three times during the visit he leaned
over to ask the director a key question: "Do you need more money for
anything?"

The director's answer was always the same one (learned in the
Washington bureaucracy). "For the programs we have, we are well
funded," he said. Finally, Representative Livingston turned to his district
representative and said, "No one ever says that to me," especially because
of his key position on the House Appropriations Committee. The congressman's next question addressed the issue of what would be needed if
a new program were funded. The answer then was that we would have to
talk about it. Could we do it with current funding, or would new funding
be required? With that, the congressman gave away what was really on
his mind and launched into the story of how all of his Louisiana-based
staff and many constituents had been to see him, insisting that "since the
federal government brought (Formosan subterranean) termites" to New
Orleans and the Gulf Coast in Asian wood crates transporting war ma-
terial and had dumped the wood into landfills, the federal government
should lead the charge in solving the problem.

One constituent who owned property in the French Quarter had
visited the Louisiana delegation in Washington, DC, on several occasions, arguing that if something was not done about the Formosan
subterranean termites (FST), there would soon be no French Quarter
because it was being eaten up! She emphasized that time was of the
essence in solving the problem.

"What can you do to help with the now overwhelming crisis?" the
congressman asked the director. The response was that SRRC did
not have any entomologists in New Orleans and only one at SRRC's
Houma, Louisiana, location. However, the director said he could lead

a major effort to develop a plan using the best university and professional researchers in the country. This would involve several universities, several federal laboratories, and personnel from industry.

When a plan was developed, the director personally delivered it to the congressman. The congressman did not open it but handed it back, saying he wanted SRRC to organize a team of experts to implement the plan. He instructed his staff to work on the issue of funding the project. The director was surprised; he felt someone else should lead the charge, but he gathered the key implementation people, again from any appropriate organization, and put the plan into action in fiscal year 1998 (see figure 5).

THE PLAN

The key players were the SRRC and three other federal laboratories, several universities, the New Orleans Mosquito Control Board (which later became the New Orleans Mosquito and Termite Control Board), and ultimately the Audubon Nature Institute (a private foundation). Universities included the Louisiana State University AgCenter (Research and Extension) (LSU), Texas A&M, University of Hawaii, University of Florida, and later the University of Mississippi and Mississippi State University.

The initial plan needed the approval of the agencies in the USDA, including the ARS, and would require the involvement of the pest-management industry, Louisiana's Department of Agriculture and Forestry, and public support. The key challenge was how to put such a diverse group together where USDA had almost no control and to handle it effectively so as to get timely results.

The plan needed a substantial core area with specific goals and relevant projects in several states. The most visible and challenging project was in the French Quarter of New Orleans. It had much concrete and macadam covering the ground (remember, these are subterranean termites) and old buildings with joint or shared walls—the toughest way to address the issue of control. A decision was made to use the French Quarter as a model, for if it could succeed there, it could succeed anywhere! To be sure, the attack would have to be an area-wide approach, not just single buildings.

With a detailed plan ready for review, a two-day cooperators' meeting was held at SRRC. Initial funding went to the LSU AgCenter for two tasks: (a) an organized approach dealing with property owners in the French Quarter, many of whom did not live in New Orleans or Louisiana, and (b) a field test on chemicals with miniature schoolhouses (about the size of a child's playhouse). Both the University of Hawaii and the University of Florida were to conduct pest-management experiments in Armstrong Park, a fairly large area with a municipal hall that borders on the French Quarter but with fewer physical constraints. Basic research was launched at the SRRC, which had added a mixed group of scientists, including entomologists, microbiologists, chemists, and engineers, and a number of construction specialists.

Additionally, demonstration and test experiments were begun in Hawaii, Florida, Texas, and Mississippi. These were places where both new research and findings discovered in other locations could be tried. Since human safety was a high priority, federal and state chemical-control agencies had to be involved. Relations with chemical companies were tried, but the issue of proprietorship became a problem in some cases.

COMMUNICATION WAS CRITICAL

To ensure that all participants were in the communications loop, a variety of mechanisms were involved. Frequent telephone calls, teleconferences, and visits to experimental sites were used, as well as e-mail. The principal mechanism, though, was cooperator meetings, which were held initially every six months to share research plans and results and discuss cooperative efforts among the team players. These were much like professional research meetings, with PowerPoint presentations, handouts, and open discussions. In time some projects came to reasonable termination points, some were extended, some were changed, and some new collaborative efforts were begun.

The key here involved two aspects: (a) joint participation of SRRC scientists and other cooperators to build a substantial research group and (b) the appointment of a national FST coordinator. His job was to oversee projects that involved non-USDA cooperators in areas such as the French Quarter and Armstrong Park and in projects in other states. He had been a member of the FST team and came from a major university. The coordinator led the semiannual (later annual) professional cooperators' meetings and was the principal contact in setting up annual public meetings, as well as meetings requested by neighborhood associations. Ultimately, the principals who worked on a daily basis in the French Quarter were the LSU AgCenter, SRRC, and the New Orleans Mosquito and Termite Control Board, often with help from the Vieux Carré Commission, an organization responsible for the French Quarter.

The concept that children might be the best (or at least a favored) way to introduce termite-management concepts to the adults in the family led to two efforts: (a) the activation of a school visitation program led by the Audubon Nature Institute and (b) school-based treatments at schools in Hawaii utilizing student involvement; specifically, a K–12 academic curriculum was designed to teach students about termite biology and principles of termite control and termite-damage prevention.

Further, the Audubon Nature Institute built an insectarium in the Old Customs Building, in which the FST display was the first to be completed. It became a very popular school visit site and an exciting stop for visitors and tourists in New Orleans.

Finally, annual brochures and periodic newsletters were distributed to citizens and civic groups to show advances in the program. Video presentations were also used. These materials were also incorporated into annual briefings to Congress and delegations, especially for the key states involved. Research results and outreach efforts were reported. TV and radio interviews were also invaluable.

One of the specific objectives in carrying out the program was to have meetings with professional pest-control operators, for these people actually did the treatments in the French Quarter and elsewhere.

HOW WAS FUNDING HANDLED?

Each project leader sat with the national FST coordinator to work out details. The principal leader was with the LSU AgCenter working through the professional pest-management operators with the concurrence of property owners in the French Quarter. This was based on the specifics used for each location. Detailed annual reports were required for each project; earlier, six-month reports had been required.

RESULTS

The initial leadership efforts were accomplished in a few months. The challenge was to develop a system to coordinate ultimately four federal laboratories, seven universities, and a private foundation, along with the New Orleans Mosquito and Termite Control Board. Fortunately, most of the FST "best brains" in the United States were involved. Around the world few laboratories have more than two scientists addressing FST. This team approach had about two and a half dozen scientists ranging from entomologists to chemists, engineers, photoelectric specialists, microbiologists, construction professionals, and communication experts.

Communication was critical to success. Frequent dialogs, site visits, regular professional meetings, reports to support groups, and periodic reports of accomplishments were provided to the Congress. Outreach to school children set the stage for a new generation of people who understand the mechanisms of FST control employing the area-wide approach. Numerous papers

were published in scientific journals, thereby sharing the results of the large, joint effort with the scientific community.
Handling of the funding followed strict guidelines and involved
detailed supervision by professional auditors.

MAJOR RESEARCH RESULTS
The major research results included the following:

1. New chemical and physical approaches to the FST problem
   were tested.
2. Even in the area of joint walls, concrete, and macadam, FST
   populations can be reduced by 50 percent within twelve to
   eighteen months.
3. Continued pressure can reduce the FST population to much
   lower figures even in heavily congested facilities in the French
   Quarter.
4. In one area that had a limited number of buildings, the results
   reduced the FST population to 3 percent of the original number. A decade after the project was initiated, former representative Bob Livingston and his staff, plus representatives of the
   principal cooperators in the French Quarter, held a celebration
   in the Waldenberg Park area, where the 97-percent reduction
   results occurred.
5. The successful area-wide approach was once again employed
   by professional pest-control operators, together with the independent evaluation provided by the LSU AgCenter.
6. A number of newer chemical approaches were tested, and
   several were found to be more satisfactory than those used in
   the late 1990s.
7. New detection approaches were developed that used audio
   systems to find concentrations of FST; infrared and related
   electronic approaches were also utilized.

8. Biological control approaches in which an organism attacks the FST show considerable promise. The challenge is to find the right approach (or combination of approaches) to kill or starve the FST colony and/or the queen.

COMMENTS

1. Today, FST are found in eleven states, and the results of this research show every indication that FST can be controlled.
2. This experiment was well funded by the Congress but provided an approach and action plan that can be used by neighborhood associations or other cities at no cost to the government. The approach has satisfied citizen groups.
3. To reiterate, the area-wide approach with a coordinating mechanism is critical to success.
4. As a result of using the scientifically based approach, the French Quarter will not be destroyed by the Formosan subterranean termite. Most of the blocks in the 128-block French Quarter are under treatment. Even areas that are not part of the current experiment are being treated at no expense to the government. To date, contracts on more than 1,560 properties are in operation.
5. With the challenge found in New Orleans, we believe that "if it can be done there, it can be done anywhere."

Leadership Perspective
The Formosan subterranean termites case study provides another example of the validity of this work's leadership model, presented in an earlier chapter. Perhaps most important was the essential cardinal virtue of Fortitude for having the ability and willingness

to confront the uncertainty and fear associated with the FST and the perseverance to see the seemingly impossible effort through. Justice proved especially important as well since many blamed the government for the initial infestation, thus yoking the USDA with accountability and responsibility for bringing it under control. Temperance and Prudence moderated the plan's formation and implementation during periods of uncertainty and great challenges.

The "important" virtues were in evidence as well. Believing came to the fore as leaders approached challenges with enthusiasm and optimism, which built and sustained trust with legislators and citizens alike. Adopting an approach that combined humility and tact ensured that those involved with the project would not underestimate the tenacity and importance of their opponent (in this case, the Formosan subterranean termite). Examples of thinking included the flexibility to create and sustain a coalition that was both able and willing to accept the challenges associated with the FST effort and able to develop a vision that was creative enough to be decisive despite the almost complete lack of precedent to guide them. In acting, the collaborators demonstrated and exploited a remarkable level of communication, bolstering their collective confidence and initiative. The resulting dynamic was one of effective assertiveness that motivated legislators and citizens and led to a solution to a problem that many viewed as exceptionally difficult and perhaps even unsolvable.

Rather than highlighting the viability of this work's leadership model in terms of the process, as we have for other case studies, we emphasize that the FST case study illustrates the efficacy of the model in terms of outcome. When paired against the implacable Formosan subterranean termite, the leadership model in this work helped secure an improbable victory in both abstract and concrete terms.

6. Gathering of the Agricultural Clan

Situation

Not infrequently, one aspect of agriculture cannot connect easily to another. This is especially true when either a natural or some other crisis leaves a void in the normal flow of information. Some states have found a way to expedite communications. A recent case involves Louisiana.

Outline

The Agribusiness Council of Louisiana joined with the Louisiana commissioner of agriculture and forestry, Louisiana State University (LSU), and the US Department of Agriculture to organize summit forums, in which a wide range of agricultural professionals are invited to meet and address issues of recovery from hurricanes or downturns in the economy.

Speakers include the commissioner of agriculture and forestry, chancellors at LSU, host institutions, experts in agricultural economics, employees in federal agencies that have helpful resources, bankers, legislators, transportation businesses, and international trade companies. Thus the forums include government (US and state) officials, members of academia, and professionals in various dimensions of agriculture (e.g., production, processing, distribution) and international trade.

Representatives of organizations and individuals who focus on specific crops or livestock breeds, as well as financial advisors, extension service specialists, political leaders, agricultural researchers, and transportation and communication specialists have all been participants.

In the summit forums, people who might not regularly interact are able to do so because of the assistance of the federal and the Louisiana state governments and the Agribusiness Council of Louisiana. Detailed minutes of the meetings are provided to each attendee after the meeting and are also placed on the Agribusiness Council of Louisiana website. Generally, there are two summit forums each year, and each has a planning committee made up of federal, state, university, and Agribusiness Council members, plus industries as appropriate to the theme of the forum.

Other dimensions of the meetings are surveys of priority issues, video recordings of the presentations, and invitational letters sent by e-mail to all interested parties. Each forum has about seventy-five attendees. The forums are held at various locations around the state, which also dictates the agenda or theme. The key issue in strengthening the agricultural economy of a relatively large area is how to bring resources together for which no one entity has specific authority.

The results of the forums are actions that are executed by the appropriate organization or individual. Additionally, there are quarterly luncheon meetings of the Agribusiness Council to focus on specific matters.

Case Study

Following Hurricane Katrina, it was not difficult to attract such a wide group of agricultural people to see how they could help one another and contribute to the recovery effort. Following Katrina, two other hurricanes (Rita and Gustave) also hit the state. Added to these natural disasters was the enormous downturn of the nation's economy in the fall of 2008. So a series of four summit forums was planned for the fall of 2008, both spring and fall of 2009, and June of 2010. The themes were as follows:

Addressing Challenges for the Future
Resilience and Recovery of Louisiana Agriculture from Recent
    Challenges
Recent Trend Impacting Louisiana in Food and Agriculture
How the Livestock Industry Is Meeting Economic Challenges

In the first forum, LSU conducted a survey of the agricultural community to identify problems and options for resolving them. Its objectives were the following:

1. Facilitate networking and communication among agribusiness leaders, higher education, and government agencies and officials.
2. Identify challenges facing the agribusiness industry and begin exploring ways to strengthen the existing infrastructure.
3. Explore the need for an agribusiness leadership institute to prepare future industry leaders.

Subsequent programs built on this base, focusing especially on the available resources and how the agriculture and food community in the state can help itself. Each forum had an organizational format: each one began with a status report (20–30 minutes) by the commissioner of agriculture and forestry (Mike Strain, DVM), comments by one of the land-grant chancellors, and remarks by a USDA leader. A keynote address set the stage for the rest of the meeting and was followed by a panel of six or seven key figures in various aspects of agriculture, such as seafood, restaurants, major commodity areas, livestock, coastal resources, finance, transportation, international trade (including the port authorities), forestry, small farms, and farmers' markets.

The resulting efforts addressed seven major issues:

How can we utilize commerce and online tools?
How can agriculture become more diversified?
How can we develop and take advantage of value-added agriculture products?
How can agriculture become more vertically integrated?
How can we develop and take advantage of niche markets?
How can we brand Louisiana agricultural products?

How can we partner with traditional and nontraditional organizations?

Even at the early stages, there have been meaningful interactions that either built on relationships that had been in existence before Katrina or occurred as a result of these forums. For example, the activities of the Louisiana Association of Cooperatives in helping farmers with business plans have increased significantly. The Port of New Orleans and chambers of commerce in various cities have become interested or involved to some extent. State legislators have joined the effort, particularly those on the legislative agriculture committees.

Time will tell how effective these efforts are, but a special retreat involving planners of the already accomplished summit forums will explore their impact and discuss possible modifications in the approach. Importantly, the commissioner's office has noted the energy that is in evidence at each forum and is considering ways to maximize it.

LOUISIANA IS NOT ALONE

Louisiana is not alone in trying to bring agricultural needs and talents together for the betterment of the agricultural economy. The Texas Ag Forum began similar efforts two decades ago to facilitate public discussion of the problems and emerging issues in Texas agriculture. It is a stakeholder-driven program in partnership with Texas Agri-Life Extension. Its goal is to educate the public on key issues affecting Texas agriculture. Like the Louisiana story, the Texas Ag Forum summarizes the presentations and programs in an annual report. In both states the focus is similar. In Texas, the emphasis is on communication; in Louisiana, it is on action.

Other states have activities that zero in on more specific issues. In California, for example, the University of California Division of Agriculture and Natural Resources has a strategic vision and addresses a wide variety of issues, such as the following:

Improve water quality, quantity, and security

Enhance competitive, sustainable food systems

Increase science literacy in natural resources, agriculture, and
nutrition

Enhance sustainable natural ecosystems

Enhance the health of California and California's agricultural
economy

Provide for healthy families and communities

Ensure safe and secure food supplies

Manage endemic and invasive pests and diseases

Improve energy security and green technologies

What is seen among the states is that the "team" approach will bring about cooperative efforts in which people with varied talents address these issues. Indeed, even where there may not be a centralized authority, people with a variety of talents and resources can work together. Certainly in the cases that involve the land-grant system, there is a centralized authority, but when others from outside the system become involved, the task grows more complex. There is real value in having the land-grant system and the state's secretary or commissioner of agriculture (and forestry or natural resources) functioning together with the USDA and the many components of agriculture for the betterment of the state's agricultural economy. However, too many targets often yield to the dispersal of limited resources, with the result that nothing happens. Focusing on specific objectives is more likely to yield a true and perhaps lasting impact.

Leadership Perspective

Building on the examples described in the previous case studies, the example of the Agribusiness Council of Louisiana provides further validation of the work's leadership model. As emphasized in the preceding case studies, collaborative efforts that involve interdepartment and/or interagency cooperation represent high-challenge leadership situations requiring adherence to the essential cardinal virtues. The efforts of the Agribusiness Council of Louisiana in the wake of numerous natural disasters again demonstrate that acting with Prudence, Justice, Temperance, and Fortitude set the conditions for successful collaborative endeavors. In addition, acting in good faith, believing in the cause, and thinking through the challenges within the parameters of the essential cardinal virtues is important and paves the ways for the successful execution of the grand idea.

While this case study provides myriad examples that support this book's leadership model, the overarching idea is that the action of communicating engenders conditions and opportunities that lead to further successes and benefits for many. It is the centrality of this effort that distinguishes this episode, provides the basis for its inclusion here, and highlights the fundamental quality of leadership necessary for all such successful endeavors: communication.

7. Monsanto: How One Company Saw the Future and Transformed to Seize It: Part 1

Prologue: Evolution into Agriculture

This case study was prepared in conjunction with the staff of Monsanto under the direction of Tamara Craig Schilling.

Based upon its original design and intent, Monsanto Company, founded in St. Louis, Missouri, in 1901 with a sole focus as a chemical producer, would have been an unlikely addition to an agricultural leadership book. For more than ninety years, the company manufactured several types of industrial, consumer, and agricultural chemicals and chemical products from saccharin to plastics and fibers to polymers. In the early 1960s, however, the company's leadership began to take a more expanded interest in chemistry applications in agriculture as farmers in the United States and abroad began to seek more advanced and mechanized ways to grow crops and control pests. Through its ag division, Monsanto produced fertilizer and herbicides, as did many other chemical-based companies during that same time. Over the next three decades Monsanto discovered and introduced several herbicides, including Ramrod, Lasso, Avadex, Harness, Machete, and Roundup, offering farmers options in controlling weeds in ways never before possible. Each of these products made important contributions to agricultural productivity around the world and placed Monsanto among the leaders in agricultural chemistry.

During the time that Monsanto's agriculture unit was developing new products, the core chemical division was continuing to thrive with both proprietary and commodity compounds, including carpet fibers, safety glass, and fire-retardant chemicals to fight forest fires. Eventually pharmaceuticals such as sleep aid Ambien, Celebrex, and the artificial sweetener NutraSweet were important contributors to this redefined life-sciences company.

By the end of the twentieth century, Monsanto, who was no

stranger to change, was squarely in the middle of its most significant transformational period. By 2002, the commodity chemicals, controls, carpets, and safety glass had been sold to other companies, and a new Monsanto, focused solely on agriculture, was spun off into its own farm-dependent entity. What emerged was an agricultural company with a handful of successful postpatent herbicides, an animal division, some newly acquired seed companies, and several biotech "traits" that promised to drastically change and improve the scope of agriculture. This newly focused and much smaller company was significantly unlike its former peers in the chemical industry and a newcomer in the long-established seed business. Monsanto had no other divisions or non-ag products on which to rely, and the future was far from clear, but the evolutionary vision had been in the minds of a few insightful leaders for many years.

Today, Monsanto is among the world's largest seed suppliers, and its chemistry efforts continue to support and enable its seeds and "traits" business. The plant biotechnology research endeavor, which began with four researchers, now comprises a crew of thousands, and the company's substantial pipeline of biotech and breeding traits promises to improve crop yields and reduce inputs at a time when farmers around the world need these technologies more than ever before.

Open to an Idea about the Future

When Monsanto first explored biotechnology in the early 1970s, the company leadership hoped that it would be a promising addition to its core chemistry business. This chapter relates how visionary leadership embraced plant science and biotechnology to transform not only the company but global agricultural production as well.

In the early 1970s Dr. Ernie Jaworski, the chemical research leader, began exploring the next strategic research and development investments. Jaworski possessed the courage required to face a couple of realities head on: many of Monsanto's then current weed-control chemistries had a limited patent life, thus requiring investment in a new chemical family discovery; in addition, the ag chemical arena was full of companies just like Monsanto, and they were all competing in the market.

Jaworski had been reading about new scientific breakthroughs in biotechnology and plant transformation that were beginning to gain momentum. He began asking questions and possessed the candor required to propose that the company explore the opportunities that plant biotechnology might bring. "We're not biologists, Ernie. We're a chemical company made up of chemists, and your job is to find and manufacture chemistries." Had Dr. Jaworski heard words to that effect, today's Monsanto would likely not be an agricultural company focused on seeds and biotech traits. It might not even exist at all if it had been absorbed into some other company, as was the case with many other firms that once competed with Monsanto in the farm chemicals arena.

Fortunately, Monsanto's leadership did not dismiss Dr. Jaworski and his team's "outside the box" thinking that crops could be transformed to tolerate herbicides even though no one in the company at that point knew how to do so. If they could not do it themselves, they would find those who could teach them. And that is exactly what they did.

In 1975, Jaworski's superiors were willing to invest some R and D into biotechnology because they could see the alignment of this interesting new science with their fledgling ag chemistry division. However, Monsanto was still very much a chemicals company with a small ag division, which, although successful, was still only a small part of the conglomerate in size and revenue. The decision to commit resources, even the modest amount that was earmarked for Jaworski's lab, was truly visionary because Roundup herbicide would not be commercialized until 1976. Few, if anyone, in the company knew then that Roundup would eventually become the blockbuster it remains today or that the Roundup Ready weed-control system would become the biotech product that would revolutionize weed control in many parts of the world and indeed in the entire seed industry. Certainly no one had planned to transform Monsanto Chemical Company into a seeds and traits corporation, but a few folks stepped forward into this exciting adjacent space. With tremendous foresight, they built upon the company's historical drive for success and harnessed the commitment to do things right while taking calculated risks to explore this intriguing opportunity.

In the 1980s, Monsanto's new CEO, Richard Mahoney, took greater steps to create potential opportunity through biology. He hired Dr. Howard Schneiderman, a biologist, as the company's chief scientist, the first nonchemist to hold that position, and charged him with hiring the talent to make essential breakthroughs. The goal was to introduce a new gene into a plant cell and grow that transformed cell into a mature plant. The company then hired its first patent attorney, who focused on protecting intellectual property rights in biotechnology. The race was on to patent new discoveries and methods of transforming plants.

Soon after Dr. Schneiderman's arrival, Steve Rogers, Rob Horsch, and Robb Fraley joined Jaworski's team and began intensive plant-based research in collaboration with leading universities. Their research led to groundbreaking achievements—the first transformed cell, followed by the first plant grown from a single transformed cell to express a new trait. They did their original work in petunias because the plant's characteristics led to a high probability of showing that the science could work. There was little if any market for transformed petunias, but the researchers were able to prove that they could grow a new plant from a single transformed cell, proving that the science of biotechnology could work.

Monsanto had a concept for the future: cross a transformed plant with a nonbiotech plant to produce seeds that contain the biotech trait. Farmers would buy the seeds from seed companies, and the company would make money. Although no one had a really clear idea on how to derive value from biotechnology-derived products, they knew that selling more Roundup was an obvious opportunity. That strategy would change drastically in the coming years as the company came to understand how to expand on the platform they were building.

The first planks in the biotech platform had been laid, and a succession of talented scientists was gradually being added to that program. Underlying the entire process was the scientists' fervent belief that plant biotechnology could be a force for good. One such scientist was Robb Fraley. Fraley grew up as an Illinois farm boy before attending college and becoming involved in molecular biology. Appreciating the challenges of farming, he signed on at Monsanto to develop biotech plant transformation but was not all that attracted to the company's quest of also selling more herbicides. He and other scientists who joined at the time believed that plants could be put to work to benefit humankind and the environment. Could utilizing plants as self-contained "factories" help reduce the use of chemical-based products or possibly reduce the consumption of natural resources?

Fraley and others at Monsanto never lost their enthusiasm for the potential of ag biotechnology, but they clearly understood they would never get to where they wanted to go without a dose of practical realism. Seasoned financial leadership within the company made it clear that these dreams of scientific breakthrough and societal contribution would not be fulfilled without a funding source. Roundup Ready crops had the potential to become the dream maker that would bring in revenue to enable future scientific exploration. Thus, researchers were inspired to leverage a plant's molecular pathway to introduce Roundup herbicide tolerance. Fast-forward to the early 1990s and building on a platform of performance and innovation: Roundup tolerance became the foundation for all future biotechnology advancements.

Plant Patents: The Intersection of Life Science and Policy
Even though Monsanto knew how to develop a herbicide molecule,

AmericanAirlines ® oneworld

RUSSIN/JOHN

CYBPBG

** NOT VALID FOR TRAVEL **
PASSENGER ITINERARY

13-JUN - THURSDAY
Baton Rouge (BTR)   655P   3438
Dallas-Ft Worth (DFW)   820P   AMERICAN AIRLINES
13-JUN - THURSDAY

San Jose, California   925P   1687   AMERICAN AIRLINES
                        1055P   AMERICAN AIRLINES

PLEASE NOTE - YOU
WILL BE REQUIRED TO
PRESENT A PHOTO ID
AT AIRPORT CHECK-IN

AmericanAirlines ®

patent it, and get regulatory approval to sell it, there was no prescription for developing or marketing a biotech trait. Then, in 1979, researchers in the pharmaceutical industry created a wave of excitement when they produced human growth hormone in bacteria. A US Supreme Court ruling in 1980 enabled a change in the government's patent program so that transformations could be patentable. Monsanto's leaders now realized that a legal structure was in place to protect biotech inventions: this opened up the possibility of creating a potential business opportunity. Jaworski's idea suddenly became more intriguing to Monsanto's leaders, who were becoming increasingly uneasy about the future stability of petroleum prices and supplies, essential components of the chemical industry.

New Capabilities for a New Opportunity

Although the company's scientists were quite excited about the promise shown thus far, for several years after the first biotech event occurred the executive management team and board of directors were interested in how to convert this scientific concept into a revenue-delivery venture. Monsanto had growth chambers full of transformed plants, but the prospect of having real products was years away. The reality of the situation was that, even though plants could be altered, the enabling techniques and tools needed to move from an isolated lab situation to a full-field application were yet to be developed, discovered, or even completely understood. Because these living plants were composed of thousands of interactive genes, the in-depth knowledge required to move this bench-level science forward became the focus of the research team. Along the way in this significant biological transformation, it was evident that many in the scientific community eagerly awaited the results of Monsanto's efforts, but various US regulatory agency leaders were examining their role in ensuring the safety and efficacy of future transformed crops for farmers and consumers. Those early agencies, farm industry groups, and company leaders paved a pathway to a system of evaluation and product stewardship that would eventually be duplicated by many countries and regions around the world.

As plant biotech developments came slowly in terms of agricultural product development, some of the early-entry companies that explored the promising science were beginning to lose their interest in spending more money in this unpredictable and undeveloped business opportunity. While some of these early start-ups closed down their work, Monsanto's scientists, academics, and biotech start-ups were convinced that they could make biotechnology a reality. However, those at Monsanto who had a promising vision of future crop development faced a major task: keeping the research funding intact by solidifying support among the chemical company's management and board members.

Collaboration Leads to Success

Early on in their journey toward real-world applications of ag biotech science, the company's technology and financial leaders knew they did not have all the answers to the complexities this exciting science offered. They also knew they did not possess all the talent and internal capabilities needed to tackle some of the challenges they would face. What they did know was that they were keenly aware that competitors were exploring similar opportunities. It became very clear that the first company to discover and develop viable biotech plants would be able to patent crucial genes and processes leading to a significant market opportunity.

The corporation resoundingly responded to the need for an "all hands on deck" approach, in which many said that Monsanto was "betting the farm" on this promising but unproven concept. In retrospect, that is exactly what it did. The concept of plant biotech had tremendous business revenue potential, but the threats and risks facing the company were arguably larger than nearly anything it had faced before. By applying the best and brightest minds to dissect the current knowledge and by building a pathway to execute the vision of transformed problem-solving crops, Monsanto declared it was on a path to define the future.

Monsanto had a public presence at many scientific and industry forums and developed relationships with leading universities. Fraley made it his job to know everything that was going on in the budding industry. The company formed collaborations of various scope and size with other researchers. To prepare to react to competitive advances by investing the intellectual resources of their established chemical organization, they were able to move more quickly to meet their objectives than many other start-up companies that were also doing cutting-edge biotech research. Major revenue and operational best practices were derived from Roundup herbicide, which continued to exhibit signs of even greater growth as innovative farmers and employees expanded the product's use into no-till, spot treatment, and farmstead markets.

A Brick and Mortar Commitment

In 1984, Monsanto opened a new $150 million research center in Chesterfield, Missouri. Monsanto now had one of the most advanced facilities in the world for aggressive research on biotechnology. It was a major addition to the company's platform, and it helped Monsanto attract top talent. The state-of-the-art facility was not just for plant genetics research; it was also used for continued work in herbicides, plant growth regulators, and pharmaceuticals after the purchase of the G. D. Searle pharmaceutical company in 1985.

By now the commitment to fund biotech was real, and so was the expectation of discovering a value-returning product relatively soon. Chief Executive Officer Dick Mahoney made it abundantly clear that the company could not and would not be able to fund biotech research indefinitely. "We are not in the business of the pursuit of knowledge," he said. "We are in the business of the pursuit of products." The intense pressure could have caused even the strongest organization to buckle, but instead it empowered the leading employees at all levels to think differently, dig deeper, and extend their reach to deliver a tangible benefit from this innovative breakthrough.

In Pursuit of a Product

Monsanto was also looking into biotechnology applications in human health, animal health, and chemical modification. However, glyphosate tolerance remained the most commercially viable possibility.

For Monsanto's ag chemical division, the new plant science research investment was being applied to expand the market opportunity with a new herbicide called Roundup. In a world of selective herbicides that controlled either grassy weeds or broadleaf weeds, Roundup was nonselective, meaning it was lethal to nearly any green vegetation but had no activity in the soil. If crops could be made tolerant to Roundup through biotechnology, could the herbicide be sprayed over the top of the crop and kill the weeds while the crop continued to grow? Back then this was a question that most farmers and herbicide industry folks would have responded to with a resounding "no." But what if it could be done? This could open new avenues for Roundup and solve tough annual and perennial weed-control challenges that farmers continued to battle. It was a big "if" but one that Monsanto's leaders wanted to explore.

It was clear that making crops resistant to glyphosate, the active ingredient in Roundup, would be the engine that would propel continued advancements. It was not just Monsanto that realized this; other ag chemical companies were pursuing herbicide tolerance as well, including glyphosate tolerance. It was unthinkable that some other company would be able to patent a transformation for resistance to the herbicide Monsanto had developed.

Based on early biotech-transformation research results, it seemed that inserting a protein into a plant cell via agro bacterium (chemical scissors) or a gene gun was a viable option in designing a Roundup-resistant or -tolerant plant. But there was one slight challenge facing the research team. What exact protein could be added to the plant to instill the resistance? And if it could be inserted in a plant, would that plant reproduce seeds? If the plant reproduced seeds, would they also carry the resistance to Roundup? If the seeds conveyed the resistance, would each seed produced have full-season and whole-plant resistance? Because farmers required a reliable and effective seed supply, these questions, although quite challenging, had to be answered. The first step required finding the protein of interest.

The company organized a full-court press to develop or modify a protein that would impart glyphosate resistance. By using their knowledge of how Roundup controlled weeds, the research team was first able to define the type of protein they were looking for. One of the not-so-obvious places to look was in Luling, Louisiana, at the Roundup manufacturing facility. In the process of testing wastewater from the production process, scientists found the gene for glyphosate resistance in a bacterium that survived in the waste stream from the plant. If they could figure out how to get crops to express the protein, farmers, instead of applying multiple herbicides for grassy weeds and broadleaf weeds, could apply Monsanto's nonselective Roundup over the top of their crop and thereby control all weeds without harming the crop. The good news for visionaries like Fraley was that Roundup had much better environmental and toxicological attributes than the multiple herbicides it could possibly replace.

Over the next few years, scientists continued to expand their knowledge and skills as they moved from the vision of plant biotech to the reality of developing a plant that would grow through an over-the-top application of Roundup herbicide. From the labs of discovery and transformation to the fields for testing, a core group of researchers focused on delivering a product to awaiting customers. During the same period, farmers were dealing with tough weed-control challenges that available chemical programs were unable to address. Increasing weed-control costs and weedy fields provided the perfect landscape for the launch of a new seed-based, weed-control program.

Regulators built the approval systems needed to ensure broad safety and use directions, and seed companies ramped up their efforts to ensure that seed would be available to customers.

Fast-forward to 1996, when farmers in the United States planted Roundup Ready soybeans for the first time. Within a few years, the first-on-the-market, biotech-treated crops would be planted on millions of acres in more than twenty countries. During that time Roundup Ready seed enabled producers who raised soybeans, corn, cotton, and canola to get improved weed control while making fewer herbicide applications. Most important, the ability to spray Roundup over the top of crops enabled farmers to increase the number of no-till acres by adopting conservation tillage practices. Because farmers have reduced the number of trips across their fields, they have saved millions of gallons of fuel, reduced the machinery wear and tear, and gained additional time. This development has conserved millions of tons of topsoil, reduced sedimentation, and kept rainfall, fertilizer, and pesticides out of streams and available to the crops. It has continued to be one of agriculture's most environmentally sustainable practices and was enabled in large measure by Monsanto's biotech seed and herbicide programs.

In the same time period Monsanto's technology organization developed a research pipeline built upon discovering and developing crop biotech traits targeted at solving significant agronomic issues and concerns with specific crop output traits. From gene discovery through regulatory approval of these novel gene events, Monsanto's scientists developed corn, cotton, and soybeans resistant to targeted insects, thereby enabling farmers to control some of the worst crop pests without using chemical insecticides.

Though it wasn't obvious at the beginning of their herbicide-tolerance research, the company leadership's push for a biotech Roundup-resistance option not only fueled the R and D financial engine but was also very compatible with the desire for ag biotech to be a force for societal good.

Monsanto: How One Company Saw the Future and Transformed to Seize It: Part 2

Change, New Technology, and New Business Model Required

Nonetheless, creating transformed crops was only part of the equation. Monsanto had produced a valuable biotech trait product, but it had yet to determine how it would get the product into the hands of farmers or charge for it as they looked for ways to recoup decades of research investment.

As the organization explored its trait distribution and compensation options, it spent significant time with seed industry experts to learn how farmers made their seed decisions. The initial approach involved licensing the Roundup Ready and YieldGard insect-protection traits via a relationship with Holden's Foundation Seed Company, which tested and distributed genetics to a few hundred seed companies across the United States, and a handful of other commercial seed businesses.

While the idea of seed biotech trait royalties was new to seed companies, the entire concept of licensing and pricing an intangible technology was completely foreign to Monsanto. This new business model offered seed companies access to biotech traits in exchange for a financial royalty for each unit of seed sold, but in the United States it also gave farmers access to the traits in the brands of seed they wanted to buy rather than limiting their choice to a small number of seed varieties. This approach would later play a major role in the overwhelming adoption rate of biotech seed acres and newly purchased soybean seed. Let us remember that seed for this year was obtained from last year's crop. In light of the patent protection afforded to the Roundup Ready soybean trait, a farmer was no longer able to save seed to plant next year. And although this was not a popular idea at the time the product was launched, within a few short years newly purchased Roundup Ready soybeans were planted on more than 90 percent of soybean acres in the United States.

With several new ideas converging at the same time that seeds containing biotech trait protection were introduced, the invested parties—farmers, seed companies, and Monsanto—were getting something out of the deal. Farmers experienced weed control like they had never seen before. They were used to buying a herbicide to apply on soybeans each year because they had done so for the past few decades. What they were not prepared for was the ability to control so many weeds that had been out of their reach before and to control them for much of the growing season—before the seed was planted until the soybean plant started to flower. Seed companies began selling soybean seed to farmers who had rarely purchased new seed beans before. In addition, many seed company representatives and agronomists enhanced their knowledge base and their service to farmers as they introduced seed with the weed and insect control in the bag, making them more influential than they had ever been. For Monsanto, revenue was coming in from both the licensing-value stream and farmers who purchased Roundup to spray on their crops. Furthermore, although the income was greatly appreciated after more than twenty years of investment in the idea, Monsanto's leaders began to realize that a new world was awaiting them if they could move deeper into the science of seed. Timing appeared more like provenance as the revenue driver, Roundup, was nearing patent expiration, allowing generic competitors to take some of the value and market opportunity Monsanto had created.

The idea of seed exploration was no longer a niche business opportunity but began to appear to be the business of the future. Leaders throughout the company began to realize that they did not understand all the intricacies of the seed business but knew they needed to if the opportunity was to be fulfilled. Ultimately they had two choices—build a full-line seed company or acquire one.

"Betting the Farm": No Going Back

Robert Shapiro, Mahoney's successor as CEO, along with Robb Fraley and Hugh Grant, were ready to make the major moves required to be a seed company, a decision that many in the company referred to as "betting the farm" to pursue a new frontier. In a two-year period beginning in 1997, Monsanto began to align its seed investments in an effort to fulfill its newfound vision.

To be a significant player in the seed market, the company had to amass a seed genetics pool to match its biotechnology pipeline. It also needed to determine where to focus its efforts to ensure it could deliver products and not just science. With its sights set on corn, soybeans, and cotton, the company purchased the number-two seed-corn company, DeKalb Genetics Corporation, and the highest-market-share soybean company, Asgrow, to acquire the global germplasm they needed to leverage the breeding side of the seed equation. Holden's Seed Company was soon added to the portfolio to enable the continued relationship with the many seed companies in the United States that had played a significant role in providing farmers access to new insect and herbicide traits.

Along with a strong genetics, Monsanto immediately had a new organization full of talented seed-industry people who understood plant breeding, market development, and sales, including the infrastructure to bring seed to farmer customers. Former chemical and pharmaceutical executives may have found themselves responsible for the new seed business, but there is no question that Monsanto's employees were prepared to be students at the feet of the newly acquired seed "trainers." At the same time, the seed company employees were ready to explore and expand the seed paradigm they were used to as they accessed the science and fed off the energy of a world-class research and development platform.

Acquiring seed companies was the final step needed to make a full commitment to agriculture and biotechnology, but the rest of the Monsanto organization was evolving as well. At this time,

Shapiro put plans into motion to fulfill what he had envisioned for a life-science company that could use biotechnology to improve crops and human health. To align along strategic growth areas, Monsanto's agricultural division, Searle Pharmaceutical, and NutraSweet businesses formed an organization whose vision was simply stated as "Food. Health. Hope." The commodity chemical business was then spun off as a single stand-alone entity called Solutia.

By 2000, blockbuster drug-discovery work was occurring in the pharmaceutical side, making it very attractive to outside suitors. At the same time, the seed-breeding and biotech pipeline was hard at work while the Roundup herbicide patent was ending. Swedish pharmaceutical company Pharmacia and Monsanto began exploring the opportunity to merge their businesses, which was an attractive option to advance the pharmaceutical pipeline. However, the merger of equals, as it was called, revealed that Pharmacia had minimal to no interest in having an ag business. It did not share the same vision of crop agriculture as Monsanto, but Monsanto's leaders maintained their belief in breeding and biotech science, along with the opportunity to provide farmers with better-yielding and resource-conserving seed. This commitment to a higher calling sustained the ag-focused organization in the months that followed as it separated from the life-science focus at Pharmacia and formed its own division—called Monsanto.

Monsanto: Same Name, New Stand-Alone Agricultural Company
The pharmaceutical industry consolidation continued with Pfizer's purchase of Pharmacia in 2002, but the huge drug company, which wanted access to Celebrex, a COX-2 drug, had no desire to maintain agricultural holdings. Thus, the Monsanto agricultural division of Pharmacia was spun off as a new, publicly traded company that focused exclusively on agriculture. This "new" Monsanto would now chart its own course but would also have to make it on its own financially. This agricultural company and its few thousand employees around the world waited to learn of the long-term direction of both

the commercial business and the research engine, and that vision would soon be painted with seed breeding and biotechnology traits at the center of their evolving future.

Monsanto's investment in seeds and biotech research expanded exponentially, receiving 95 percent of the company's annual R and D budget as of 2010. Leveraging this significant sum, Monsanto's researchers sought ways to radically change the historical development, assessment, and analytical methods used in crop breeding. Traditional plant breeding required growing crops to maturity, scouting fields for the best-looking phenotypes, breeding from those parents, and repeating the process in subsequent seasons until new hybrids or varieties were ready for market. It was a time-consuming practice that relied on judgments derived from what someone saw in the field.

While many seed companies were still using their eyes to develop products, Monsanto, as a newcomer to the field, looked at new approaches to breeding. It sought to bring science to bear by nondestructively analyzing the DNA in each seed the breeders produced. Again, leadership sought automation and robotics tools to develop high-throughput methods of analyzing the DNA of individual seeds. Monsanto's in-house staff designed and constructed their inventions. One significant development is the seed chipper, which allows researchers to chip a small sample off millions of seeds each year, analyze the DNA in those samples, plant only the seeds with the desired characteristics, and feed the information into a data network for analysis by plant breeders all over the world. This high-throughput science application has not only reduced the normal field-testing time and increased the speed of seed-variety development but also improved the trait-transformation process and enabled the collection of major points of data that can be leveraged via predictive models. The technology organizations' employees at all levels continued to develop innovative ways to bring new products to market faster than ever before—all in an effort to provide farmers the seed they needed to manage their inputs (e.g., water, pesticides) to improve crop production.

A Sustainable Yield Commitment

Today, via the seeds Monsanto sells through its own brands, including DeKalb, Asgrow, Channel, and Seminis, as well as various other companies' brands globally, it continues to explore opportunities to increase productivity for the producer who purchases them. Productivity shows up in many ways through tons, bushels, and bales of crop yield, as well as taste, crop quality, and nutritional value. Its seeds are also intended to conserve the resources (e.g., land, water, energy, fertilizer) required to produce crops, with the ultimate goal of minimizing the environmental impact of each crop unit produced.

The final component of this seed company's vision is to develop seed systems that enhance not only the tangible side of crop production but also the intangibles of farmers' lives, whether their farm consists of a hectare in Asia or many sections of land in the Americas. Even though intangibles are sometimes difficult to assess, farmers from all parts of the world have experienced the impact of higher-output and/or lower-input seed on their lives, including more time to spend with family, more opportunity to bring future generations into their operation, or more income at the end of the year to enable them to purchase a home or send their children to school. Although these things may seem basic to many, the effects brought about by the advent and adoption of such seed are not evident at first, but they are real and have been captured through farmers' stories all over the world.

However, as farmers have benefited from these enhancements, Monsanto has been intensely aware that it, too, must be able to profit from its R and D investments. One term that has been commonly used in the past decade to describe the sharing of this increased opportunity is "value capture," which means that a company like Monsanto captures the value of the breeding and biotech products it has developed as a portion of the incremental gain to farmers when they plant the seed the company produces.

The Value of Seed and Trait Innovation

Monsanto's philosophy has been to price products to share in the value that it provides to farmers through reduced input costs, higher yields, and more. This concept of capturing value from each one of the millions of acres where the seeds are planted has been a new approach for the seed industry. In essence, value capture works on the premise that the new seed, which likely contains proprietary genetics and biotech traits, will create a benefit significantly greater than that produced by systems the farmer utilized in the past. In addition, with the corn, soybean, cotton, and canola biotech-traited genetics, this has been the case as yields have increased incrementally each year while inputs like pesticides and fuel have gone down per unit of crop produced.

However, we must keep in mind that, although the logic and the scientific quantification make total sense, cultural norms and governmental polices also play in role in assessing the value and thus the income that should be derived from the sale of a specific product. Value capture has been one of the most challenging issues Monsanto has faced in several parts of the world, but it is potentially underestimated by many who knew of the benefits of better-producing seed.

As a chemical company, Monsanto followed a simple sales model: make chemical products, and customers will buy them if they see the value. Each resin or pharmaceutical or fiber was made the same way as the last, and if they met the needs of the buyer, they were sold, and more were produced with the original recipe. The model was very similar even in the agriculture chemical industry, where a gallon of Roundup or Lasso herbicide was made with the same formula basically the way the last batch was made; it performed just as the last gallon did; and, if demand increased, another batch could be manufactured. But the biological and cultural reality of seed production and planting was different.

The historical practice of using seed from the prior year's crop to plant this year's crop is especially significant in soybeans and grains such as wheat. When bringing Roundup Ready soybeans to market in 1996, Monsanto knew it would need to develop a system whereby growers would agree not to save seeds that contained patented biotech traits. Otherwise, the return on the company's years of investment would be limited to a one-time sale, and the vision of a technology pipeline would vanish. Most growers around the world realized that the benefits of the new weed-control program were worth purchasing new seed every year, but the approach caused resentment in some customers.

In the United States, Monsanto had the support of patent law and seed-industry infrastructure to bring a highly valuable but intellectual property-dependent product to the market. The law upheld the right for Monsanto to expect farmers not to replant seed they saved from year to year; more important, producers and the seed-distribution chain quickly saw the benefits that investment in innovation could bring through better weed control, increased yields, and reduced herbicide costs in Roundup Ready soybeans. However, a small percentage of farmers felt that once they purchased a bag of soybeans, the resulting production was theirs, and they had the right to replant the soybeans they saved if they chose, no matter what the US patent office or their Monsanto grower agreement said. And in some cases, this very thing happened.

Early after the launch of Roundup Ready soybeans, Monsanto knew it was being tested. Would it uphold its legal rights and secure the funding for its R and D pipeline, or would it look the other way to avoid conflict with its farmer customers? In reality, farmers who were not saving Roundup Ready soybean seed from year to year made the decision much clearer. Farmers who wanted the future investment in seed technology and were purchasing new soybean seed each year made it clear to Monsanto's sales organization and company leaders that they expected the company to follow through on its commitment in the grower agreement to keep the playing field level. In essence, farmers themselves expected Monsanto to keep other farmers from saving soybean seed to ensure that all farmers were paying for the technology from which they were benefiting.

Although this seems like a pretty simple request on paper, the impact of a major industry shift took not only time but also a different perspective in light of the fact that agriculture in the United States had traditionally been a way-of-life business built on integrity. Moreover, the overwhelming majority of farmers kept their side of the bargain, but the few who did not faced scrutiny by those who were investigating seed-piracy claims. From the time Monsanto began selling herbicides to the present day, it has been committed to supporting its farmer customers. Additionally, the decisions it had to make and the processes it implemented to aggressively enforce grower licensing agreements were very difficult, but fifteen years later, millions of farmers continue to invest in the enhanced genetics and biotech traits that have come out of the pipeline and have benefited from the investments they make each year when they buy new seed.

The business model in Argentina and other parts of South America was not quite so simple. Monsanto's expectation of patent protection requiring farmers to purchase new seed to access Roundup technology was dashed when the Argentinean government and courts decided differently. With the country's proximity to the southern portion of Brazil and access to the biotech trait, Argentina's "brown-bag" Roundup Ready seed moved across the border years before it was deregulated in Brazil. At the same time, producers in the United States were investing in the new technology; their South American peers were gaining access to this new weed-control option without paying into the opportunity it offered. This volatile dynamic revealed the realities of doing business globally, where policies and regulations vary.

The company was at a critical crossroads. One direction was simpler in some ways—it could continue to bring seed genetics and traits to the market, knowing farmers would replant them and buy only a portion of new seed each year to obtain some income. The other, more contentious track required the company to pursue the situations in which farmers were saving seed. Doing so would certainly be confrontational, but upholding intellectual-property patent protection remained the cornerstone of Monsanto's technology vision. Pursuing the second path was the only real option if Monsanto wanted to secure the vision it had put into motion many years before.

Execution of patent protection showed up in the United States in the pursuance of seed-piracy settlements where possible, which farmers and the company have expected as a necessary norm. The international dynamics have proven to have varied impacts based on decisions made and actions taken by all of the players involved. Inability to slow the illegal Argentinean seed movement spurred the company to close down its soybean operations. Brazil's government and grain buyers, however, agreed to postharvest testing and trait fee collection, so investment in corn, soybean, and cotton research in the country continued.

While a small group of dissenters has attempted to hype the impact of Monsanto's actions over the years, the vast majority of farmers and industry organizations have supported this challenging but important demonstration of leadership. Farmers who save the biotech seed and replant it the following year face charges of patent infringement and basically seed piracy, a form of intellectual property theft. In essence, the farmers who invested in the technology reaped the benefits of this value-sharing and patent-protection approach.

The Reality of Public Opinion

In reflection, Monsanto did not realize that its quest to reduce pesticide use and apply biotechnology to seed production to make farming more sustainable would not resonate with everyone. For more than two decades, the company's goal has been to help provide abundant food for a growing population and a healthy environment for future generations. A significant observation has resulted in the awareness that the company was likely so focused on this objective that it was not sufficiently cognizant of human nature to question innovation regardless of the amount of scientific proof of safety and societal benefit.

What might be one of the company's unexpected findings in the long drive to technological success is that Monsanto fell prey to antibiotech activism. Public concern and reaction have entered the dialogue around the widespread adoption of biotechnology to the detriment of sustainability. Highly focused activist opponents raised unfounded fears about the products the company has created. Those products have provided tremendous benefits to farmers, their surrounding communities, and the environment, yet there are some objections to this approach.

Beyond the Bag: Seed-Driven Solutions

Developing pricing strategies that offered significant benefit to the crop producers while generating enough income to the company was a vexing part of the business and would require considerable understanding of pest infestations, dialogue with farmers about their expectations, and creative thinking to explore the potential advantages.

Seed-corn technology continued to provide farmers substantial value, but the value-share equation played out a bit different since farmers who had converted to hybrid seed did not save seeds from their crop. In open-pollinated corn production, only some kernels contained the desired superior genetics, but others would not, so millions of farmers around the world moved to hybridized corn, which required pollination. This type of production alleviated the situation of saved seed; however, other challenges that affected pricing emerged for the young seed company. For example, a corn seed with built-in insect protection was highly valued when insect pressure was high but was not valued at the same level by the customer in years when insect infestations were lighter. In the same way that seed companies historically priced genetics based on performance, Monsanto trialed a new concept of pricing corn-insecticide traits across regions based on the average, but variable, pest damage by area.

Drought-tolerant corn, a major segment of Monsanto's technology effort, would require major consideration before this revolutionary product could be priced. Throughout the United States alone weather patterns varied so greatly from year to year and within a zone or geographic area. While a drought-prone hybrid or variety has greater value to a farmer in an unusually dry season, no one knows what the exact conditions will be before the growing season starts. The complexity of the situation might have overwhelmed agronomists who were faint of heart, but the quest to bring the next game-changing seed technologies kept the Monsanto team focused on figuring out the scientific and economic mechanisms required to make them a future reality.

Another example of creative thinking came in 2007, when a group of Monsanto product-marketing managers began considering the risk-reduction impact of corn biotech traits based on farmers' anecdotes and observations. After in-depth evaluation with esteemed academicians and insurance actuaries, the team had clear evidence via thousands of summarized yield reports that YieldGard Bt rootworm and corn borer insect-protection products offered a valuable risk-management tool for farmers. The project leaders took their risk-protection concept to the USDA's Risk Management Agency with a request that it offer crop-insurance rate reduction to biotech insect-protected corn adopters. After thorough review and revision, the USDA developed the Biotech Yield Endorsement pilot program, which provided farmer users with a reduced insurance premium for their seed investment.

Collaboration as a Core Competency

Bringing value to farmer customers so they could produce more food and reduce their impact on the environment was Monsanto's vision of sustainable agriculture based on its 2008 commitment to deliver a doubling of yields by 2030. Monsanto's researchers continue to discover new traits, but they also are aggressively collaborating with other companies to develop new options that will help address the critical need to produce more food while reducing environmental impact. The company understands that it is not able to address the great global need by itself but that it can work together with others who share a similar vision.

CEO Mahoney's famous words of developing a product instead of collecting knowledge was only half right. Monsanto had to have a product, or its dreams of a biotech future would perish. But it has never stopped collecting knowledge. Collaboration is a key to the company's continued success. It finds talents that can augment its employees' own abilities. No one at the old Monsanto knew how to analyze DNA, identify marker genes, discover new proteins, or manufacture analytical equipment that would enable them to screen millions of seeds per year. All of these capabilities were essential to their success, and the company either sought out or developed all of them. Monsanto is a magnet for the best and brightest employees because they understand the company's commitment to its vision for a better world.

However, not only are farmers and employees attracted to the results of Monsanto's vision, but companies and organizations of all types and sizes and with a variety of interests have found commonality with the agricultural organization. Whether aligning with another company, university, industry group, or scientific organization, Monsanto has an intense desire to link with others who can add innovative thinking, techniques, and science to advance the cause of greater farm productivity. The company has determined that the value of building relationships and networks goes far beyond the cliché and is a core focus that greatly surpasses the "not invented here" mindset. Instead, the openness to partnerships of various kinds sparks the innovative vein running through the company.

Seizing New Opportunities

Current CEO Hugh Grant continues to drive Monsanto's position in seeds and biotechnology as he leads the company through the complexities of the world's largest and most elemental industry: agriculture. Corn, soybeans, cotton, and canola remain the core row crops, but the company has added vegetables, sorghum, wheat, and sugarcane to its portfolio as it explores future growth opportunities.

In addition to developing crops that help farmers, Monsanto is now moving in the direction of more healthful foods that will benefit consumers directly. It anticipates regulatory approvals for soybean oils, including those that are low in trans fats and saturated fats, which should yield more healthful french fries or other products made with soybean oil. It has also developed a soybean that delivers heart-healthy omega-3 fatty acids conveyed through its oil.

These products continue to fulfill the vision of the young molecular biologist Dr. Robb Fraley, who joined Monsanto so many years ago with hopes of developing a new, viable agricultural science called biotechnology.

No Greater Cause than Delivering on a Vision

Great challenges lie ahead for agriculture. Farmers around the world must double food production in the next forty years to meet population demand. The world must conserve precious resources, especially water, soil, and energy. These challenges create opportunity, and Monsanto's goal is to continually prepare to deliver on its part of that future.

Monsanto emerged as the leader in agricultural productivity and in seed and plant biotechnology for a number of reasons:

While taking calculated risks to explore a new field of uncertainties, it built on a preexisting platform. Monsanto had an agricultural division, so it had an understanding of agriculture's producers, markets, needs, and challenges and was willing to use a "paradigm lens" to explore potential opportunities.

It used its financial and human resources to stay the course in developing useful products via a new science. The successful chemicals business provided financial resources that enabled Monsanto to spend many years researching a new field that was related to one of its core competencies.

Its business leaders took a step-by-step approach to embracing plant biotechnology. Each step had some risk, but until the final commitment was made, there was always room to retreat to the company's existing businesses if necessary.

Monsanto's business leaders were practical; ideas were one thing, but they knew that none of the vision could be achieved without a profitable product concept approach to sustain the company.

They practiced good science and employed researchers who believed they could make the necessary breakthroughs. This created an exciting environment for talented people who wanted to work at Monsanto to fulfill the vision.

Monsanto harnessed the benefit of being new to the seed industry. It was not locked into doing things the way they had always been done. The company explored new ways of developing products and was innovative in building the technology pipeline.

It was driven by a vision to increase the production of crops that required fewer inputs while positively affecting the lives of farmers and society at large. This view of sustainable agriculture was and remains Monsanto's ultimate quest.

Some might believe that Monsanto's evolution to a company focused solely on agriculture happened by chance, but a group of insightful company leaders over the years was willing to "bet the farm" on the future science and opportunity of seed and plant biotechnology. Its legacy will live on through the farmers who have invested their lives to feed, fuel, and clothe our world.

Leadership Perspective

The Monsanto case study provides a different type of support for the values of this book's essential cardinal virtues. Fortitude, Justice, and Temperance became the watchwords of Monsanto's drive to become a leader in its field and elucidate the essential goodness at the very core of its efforts. Eschewing the profit motive of simply "selling more herbicides," the partners in this case study coalesced around the twin notions "that green plants could be put to work to benefit humankind and the environment" and "that plant biotechnology could be a force for good," thus establishing a tremendously powerful foundation for their soon-to-be groundbreaking advances in biotechnology and chemistry. Their platform of good intentions benefited many and attracted numerous other good people and organizations to their cause, which in turn provided the partners with more resources and opportunities to achieve their objectives.

Thinking was most evident in their vision and creativity, which, when coupled with their acting with integrity and confidence, motivated others to join them, believe in their optimism, and allow for the emergence of change agents in several areas. Perhaps more than any other case study here, the Monsanto example illustrates the potential synergy of the elements of this work's leadership model. It shows that the "essential" and "important" elements can combine to produce (or allow for the emergence of) results with value far beyond the sum of the whole.

This, in essence, is the fundamental argument of this book: leadership based on the timeless cardinal virtues and conducted in ways of thinking, acting, and believing in concert with the cardinal virtues is tremendously effective and powerful regardless of whether applied in the wake of natural disasters, in the midst of entrenched political influence, or in the complex environment of the world's free-market economy. Principled leadership based on solid values and conducted in honorable ways makes the difficult attainable and the impossible achievable.

8. Enhancing Leadership in the State Agricultural Experiment Stations

Situation

Prior to initiation of the Experiment Station Committee on Policy (ESCOP) Leadership Development Program, there were no formal leadership-development opportunities available to personnel in the state agricultural experiment stations. If individuals wanted to enhance their leadership skills, they were required to seek leadership training in another venue.

What Will This Case Study Show?

This case study illustrates the significance of identifying and resolving an important issue from the time the issue is realized or conceived until it is resolved. From the beginning, it was envisioned that programs for emerging leaders were needed at the professor, associate dean/director, dean/director, or vice president's level in academic agricultural sciences.

Case Study

Those involved in agricultural programs in academia (primarily land-grant universities) have long recognized the importance of leadership in the discharge of agriculture-related responsibilities. Beginning at the entry level in research, a scientist may be referred to as a "project leader." This denotes that the person must possess some level of leadership skill and ability.

By design, the US Agricultural Research System in land-grant universities involves many and varied types of cooperators and collaborators, all requiring skilled leadership to be successful. Administrators at all levels long recognized that there was no mechanism for developing and/or enhancing leadership skills among newly employed scientists and especially new administrators. The newly appointed project leader was often responsible for managing substantial funds (from thousands to millions of dollars), several faculty and staff members, and considerable equipment. More often than not, these individuals had received no formal training in any aspect of leadership. The exception was the rare individual who had been in military ROTC or received some other leadership experience.

For project leaders, the situation was serious. However, for others at higher levels, it was even more critical. Department heads, experiment station directors, and agricultural college deans were often appointed even though they might have had no formal training in leadership. It was truly on-the-job training, sometimes with unfortunate outcomes.

This was the situation at the time ESCOP created a "special initiatives committee," which identified a number of opportunities for ESCOP to strengthen the "system" and advance the agricultural research agenda in the United States.

One of the committee's ideas was to develop a means of enhancing the leadership skills of scientists and administrators in the state agricultural experiment stations. ESCOP accepted the report of the special initiatives committee and voted to support and implement the recommendation on enhancing leadership in the system. Then ESCOP quickly appointed a committee to develop more definitive plans to implement such a program.

SETTING THE STAGE: THE CURRICULUM

Once the committee and the chair of the committee were appointed, the chair developed a "straw man" to begin discussion on the implementation of a leadership development program. The committee's first reaction was that "it had not been done before," so it probably could not be done or was not worth the expense or effort. Another prevailing opinion (though often not verbally expressed) among most of the experiment station directors was that "we were good enough already and didn't need any leadership training." The committee debated this issue at great length.

Finally, it was realized that the charge by the chair of ESCOP was not to revisit ESCOP's decision; rather, it was to develop an implementation plan for enhancing leadership within the state agricultural experiment stations. With this simple premise, the committee began to make progress in developing a plan.

The group agreed that a leadership development program was a sound idea and that the effort should include not only experiment station personnel but also cooperative extension and teaching personnel from the entire agricultural academic environment. The committee members explored this idea in great depth but finally and reluctantly abandoned it when they were vigorously rebuffed by both the cooperative extension and the teaching leadership.

Then came the serious work of developing a concept that each member of the small committee could agree on. This was no easy task. For example, some wanted the program to be a relatively undemanding course. Others, however, envisioned a much more rigorous program, with each day beginning at 5 a.m. with physical exercise and culminating in a mandatory study hall in the evening and a formal lights-out at 10 p.m. Fortunately, there was sufficient compromise to permit agreement on a middle-ground outline.

The discussion about the outline and specific content of the program was just beginning. Committee members quickly agreed that there should be some linkage with or sharing by administrators who were supporting their participant's involvement in the program.

Consequently, in addition to the formal instruction, the committee members proposed a highly flexible, independent activity that would be carried out under the direction of the participant's administrator at home. As things turned out, the individual activity took many forms, and the result was a wide array of projects completed under the auspices of the ESCOP Leadership Development Program and directed by the participant's experiment station director or administrator.

The specific topics to be included in the basic or initial phase were finally selected by a professional leadership development group. The utilization of such a service proved to be a stroke of genius inasmuch as the committee worked out the seemingly unsolvable problem of what subjects to include in the formal instructional phase by working cooperatively with the professional leadership group.

All of those involved soon agreed to run the course in three phases: Phase I would be a resident phase, and phase II would give the participants "hands-on" experience related to course work from phase I. Phase II would be completed at the home station under the supervision of the participant's director or the director's designee. Phase III was to be a Washington, DC, experience.

Phase I comprised three sections:

1. Self-assessment using the Myers-Briggs and other tests
2. Fundamentals and implementation of leadership
3. Implementing Leadership

Fundamentals of leadership included the following:

principles of leadership
values and ethics in leadership
problem solving and the decision-making process
communication for effective leadership
motivation for maximum productivity
managing conflict through negotiation
managing stress

Implementing leadership included the following:

group and individual dynamics
role of strategic planning
power, politics, and the art of persuasion
crisis management

A final part of phase I dealt with the genesis and evolution of the land-grant university system and the state agricultural experiment stations. Specific topics included the following:

a historical perspective of the land-grant university
the Hatch Act (which authorized a national system of State Agricultural Experiment Stations, along with related legislation)
contemporary sociology and philosophy of science, priority setting, and program planning in the state agricultural experiment stations
the role of the state agricultural experiment station administrator

Phase II (to be completed at one's home station) was designed to develop rapport with the SAES director and administrative staff; convey an understanding of the function and role of the decision makers in the administration of a land-grant university and to impart knowledge and an appreciation of middle management of the university, especially subject matter units (departments). Also, participants were expected to gain knowledge and a perspective of a station's involvement in regional research and to develop an understanding of the roles of various support units of the experiment station, including communications, business office, EEO officer, experimental design group, grants and contracts office, and other supporting groups.

The series culminated with phase III—the "Washington experience." This phase included a myriad of topics designed to provide participants a better understanding of how the federal government is involved in agriculture, particularly in research.

Another valuable asset of the professional leadership-development group was that it included several excellent instructors.

Once a curriculum was established, the issue of logistics became relevant. Since the committee did not have a budget of any kind and by design was not interested in grants,[2] the question of financing became a sensitive topic.

Concurrently, the committee located a facility that for a single fee would provide lodging, food, and meeting rooms with audio visual support and so on. This single cost per participant, as well as the cost of the professional training group, enabled the committee to arrive at a fixed cost per participant for the course. This let administrators know exactly what each participant's cost would be.

BEGINNING THE COURSE: ATTRACTING UP-AND-COMERS

The arrival of participants for Class 1 was met with great apprehension. In order to facilitate instruction, participants were assigned to teams—red, blue, and green. There were obviously many questions. However, after the first day, there was such enthusiasm that the members of the ESCOP Leadership Development Committee, including the chair, decided to assign themselves to one of the teams, where they functioned as participants in the instruction along with the registrants from around the county.

One of the many unanticipated benefits of the program was participant networking. There were many opportunities to share experiences, and this enabled the strengthening of the entire system. Many of these interactions led to strong friendships.

By the end of Class 1, the chair and some members of the Leader Development Committee felt "burned out" and asked to be relieved of their assignment. It had been an unusual committee assignment with an inordinate amount of work, which was unlike most committee assignments. However, participation in this effort proved to be fulfilling.

OUTCOMES: BROADENING THE BASE

The ESCOP was pleased with the outcome of the first class, and after a round of accolades for the chair and members of the committee, quick action was taken. The ESCOP chair appointed a new chair of the leadership and development effort and replaced the departing committee members.

Although the consensus was that the participants in the class indeed benefited from the experience, both the committee and the participants realized that such a leadership program was quite valuable and would pay large dividends for the experiment station system in the future. In essence, most of the participants became advocates for the program. Also, because the program involved the experiment station directors, who paid their participants' fees in the effort, they became knowledgeable and were for the most part supportive.

Over the years, it seems that each new chair and committee member brought new ideas that continually improved and strengthened the program. There were several significant developments. First was incorporating teaching faculty through the Academic Committee on Policy (ACOP). Later, the Extension Committee on Policy (ECOP) decided to merge its own effort, National Extension Leadership Development (NELD), which initially had been supported by the Kellogg Foundation, with the ESCOP-ACOP program. Out of the merger came a new leadership development program that serves faculty in all three functions: research, teaching, and extension. Thus was born LEAD-21, Leadership for the Twenty-First Century, which is still in place.

Starting in June 2010, LEAD-21 hosted class six. Concurrent with the creation of LEAD-21 and quite coincidentally, land-grant university leaders and the Association of Public Land-Grant Universities (APLU) (a new name for NASULGC) saw a need for more advanced leadership development to support agricultural college administrators who aspired to upper-level university positions. This realization resulted in a Kellogg Foundation grant awarded to North Carolina State University, Ohio State University, and the University of Vermont to develop the Food Systems Leadership Institute (FSLI), which started its sixth cohort in October 2010. The Land-grant University System is now well served by two leadership development opportunities: LEAD-21 as the introductory program and FSLI as the more advanced program.

The ESCOP leadership development course and later the ESCOP-

ACOP course were conducted for fourteen years. During this time more than fourteen hundred participants completed the program. Participants represented most states, scientific disciplines, and various nationalities and included both men and women, thus reflecting the great diversity of personnel in university agricultural academic programs.

While a number of graduates of the program have accepted leadership positions in the system or elsewhere, there have been numerous other benefits as well. Space does not provide an opportunity to describe each of the individual projects. However, there were a number of very impressive efforts such as the creation of research centers, new research facilities, and innovative research programs. For example, at the University of Georgia two projects were the creation of the Center for Soybean Improvement and the National Environmentally Sound Production Agriculture Laboratory (NESPAL), which can be traced back to the leadership program. Both are still strong entities at UGA today.

While a complete assessment has not been done, it is clear that these programs have achieved a remarkable degree of success. Essentially all graduates of the program have indicated that the curriculum has had a positive impact on their careers. In fact, the first chair of the ESCOP Leadership Development Committee enjoys office space in the NESPAL facility.

Graduates of the various leadership development programs now serve in many leadership positions in the agricultural academic community, as well as in industry, government, and other agricultural venues. This includes a number of department heads in the academic environment and research leaders in other organizations. Also, many graduates serve as directors, associate or assistant directors of agricultural experiment stations, the Cooperative Extension Service, and academic institutions. Other graduates serve as executive officers of scientific societies, and a number of graduates have accepted positions of greater responsibility in government, particularly the USDA.

It is especially noteworthy that graduates of the ESCOP Leadership Program are serving in numerous senior administrative positions in the nation's two- and four-year institutions, as well as graduate institutions, including 1862 and 1890 land-grant universities. Indeed, some graduates have served as presidents of the nation's leading land-grant universities and other major institutions that offer agricultural programs.

A sound argument could be made that this acceptance of positions of greater responsibility cannot be directly attributed to the success of the leadership development program. However, it would be reasonable to assume that individuals who aspired to positions of greater responsibility would seek out means of strengthening their leadership skills. In any event, the system is the beneficiary of their enhanced leadership ability.

The overwhelming majority of participants in the various leadership development programs appear to be convinced of the value of the program. Here are a few selected comments by participants:

"This was a life-changing experience. I am a different person after being a part of this group. Everyone in a leadership situation deserves to be a part of this program."

"This leadership program has been very stimulating and most rewarding. It has far exceeded whatever hopes I might have had."

"I have gained an appreciation of the complexity of the challenges facing leaders at higher levels of university administration and also the sense of my own abilities and skills."

From a participant's administrator—"Our participant has developed more confidence in his administrative abilities. He has a unique ability to deal with a wide range of personalities and opinions and moves to logical outcomes."

Although the consensus was that the initial leadership development effort had been successful, the original committee had visions of a much broader effort in leadership development for the state agricultural experiment stations. The committee started by conducting an opinion survey relative to future leadership course offerings by ESCOP. Courses suggested included an orientation course for department heads, an SAES leadership development course for administrators, and an orientation course for directors called "Making the Political Process Work for the SAES." Results of the survey revealed considerable support for a much broader leadership development effort in the SAES; however, the environment at that time precluded acting on these suggestions.

Given the challenges that confront agriculture today, we believe that leadership development throughout agriculture, especially in the academic area, needs to be strengthened. Although academic excellence is vital, leadership skills are also a necessity for the future success of the agricultural enterprise.

RESULTS

Personal responses of graduates of the program have been very positive.

A significant percentage of graduates have accepted greater responsibility in the experiment station system and even higher levels in academia.

The original mission of the ESCOP Leadership Development Program has not only survived but is also now embraced by LEAD-21, which includes the Cooperative Extension Service and agricultural academic programs.

Leadership Perspective

Applying this book's leadership model to the formation of a leadership development course for agriculture (in this case, that of ESCOP) provides a wonderful opportunity to examine the model as implemented by other leaders seeking to enhance leadership abilities within their own organizations. The examples of Prudence and Fortitude are quite evident, as it made sense to deliberately develop their own leaders and to persevere in the effort to do so in spite of the naysayers, but the thinking associated with creating and implementing the vision for the program was perhaps the most important element of all. This program required many to act with initiative and to motivate others to support their efforts. In the end, however, it was likely the efforts associated with believing that made the program a success in that the trust placed in the participants was justified by the outcomes: the participants became highly capable and successful individuals who garnered respect for themselves and the program and worked for the benefit of many involved in the program and far beyond its sphere of influence.

Using a leadership model to analyze the efforts to establish and implement a leadership development program may well be the most persuasive validation of an abstract concept, and this case study indicates that this work's leadership model is indeed useful, if not essential, in such efforts.

9. Development of the Council for Agricultural Science and Technology

Introduction

This case study illustrates the myriad of challenges associated with developing an organization that embraces many groups, individuals, and scientific disciplines. In the late 1960s science and technology began placing increasing pressure on agriculture. The publication of books such as *Silent Spring* had called attention to the widespread use of pesticides and their potentially harmful side effects. The use of antibiotics in animal feed had become an accepted agricultural practice with potentially undesirable outcomes. Unfortunately, as these kinds of issues became popularized, individuals and groups got involved and began challenging them and developing responses with little appreciation for scientific rigor.

Evidence was mounting that there must be an effective means of providing sound, science-based information about the science and technology of agriculture to the media, the US Congress, and the public at large. Although individual institutions and scientific societies are effective in responding to many local and technical aspects of science issues directly related to their location or discipline, many issues could be more effectively addressed by a multidisciplinary approach representing a number of institutions. For example, many science-based issues in agriculture required an economic and sociological perspective. Other issues require a legal perspective.

At the time there was no mechanism for effectively and efficiently convening a multidisciplinary task force to address a given problem or issue in any aspect of agriculture. The Council for Agricultural Science and Technology (CAST) was conceived as a means of addressing issues that were difficult, if not impossible, for an individual scientific society or institution to address. There was never any intent for CAST to compete with or engage in activities that could best be handled by an individual scientific society or a single institution.

Over the years CAST has made many minor changes in how it addresses issues; however, it has consistently received praise and recognition for its contributions to agriculture. In recent years, especially in the down economy, the business model has failed to generate the support required to maintain the operation. The real challenge is to develop a stronger commitment on the part of those who have a responsibility for the science and technology of agriculture.

Situation

This case study illustrates the challenge in leadership to bring together representatives from multiple scientific societies and disciplines and a wide array of organizations and institutions. It also shows how, as conditions change, the organization needs to change as well. Effective leadership is the key to responding to these challenges. In response to these perceptions and situations, the National Research Council of the National Academy of Sciences convened a planning committee to consider this state of affairs. From this effort emerged a group of visionary individuals in the agricultural science community representing various scientific societies who agreed with the committee's findings and initiated action to address this situation. Although a few administrators took part in this effort, industry scientists and university faculty members accomplished much of the work.

The Challenge

A major concern has to do with how a broad section of the agricultural science community can come together and address common issues. Around the middle of the twentieth century, the rapid escalation of science and technology in agriculture was outstripping the public's understanding and, more important, its appreciation of agricultural science and technology.

This was recognized as particularly important for the public, the news media, and members of the US Congress. The issue was even more challenging because some groups and organizations opposed certain aspects of technology in agriculture, such as the widespread use of pesticides. These groups often responded on an emotional basis. Their actions and positions lacked scientific rigor.

The Idea

In December 1970, Nyle C. Brady, then chair of the Agricultural Board, Division of Biology and Agriculture, National Research Council, National Academy of Sciences, convened a meeting in Washington, DC, of the council to discuss "The Role of Agricultural Scientific Societies" in agriculture. Representatives from sixteen agriculturally related scientific societies met to discuss the creation of a new organization that would provide accurate scientific information about agricultural issues involving science and technology to decision makers in government, the media, and the public at large. Brady likely was the first person who had the vision to move the discussion of such a diverse group to coalesce around a common goal. Obviously, the objective was to create an organization to address important issues from a multidisciplinary perspective. The group named the organization the Council for Agricultural Science and Technology, and it was chartered as a nonprofit 501(c)(3) organization in 1972.

Several scientific societies quickly accepted the arguments regarding the merit of this undertaking. However, there was critical concern about some aspects of the new organization. Scientific societies sometimes reflect competing interests in agriculture and also have strong nonagricultural components among their membership. Some have a solid commitment to the basic sciences and a lesser one to applied or practical concerns. Thus, it was necessary to match shared interests with specific society goals and agendas. In common language, it takes a broader vision to make a commitment for the greater good than for the specific goals of one society or institution.

Specific challenges associated with the need for an organization such as CAST included the tremendous increase in a wide array of emerging new technologies in agriculture, particularly pesticides, growth regulators, and antibiotics associated with animal production. New technologies were a part of specific agricultural disciplines. While each scientific society (discipline) could respond to such difficulties, often a response from a broader approach was more effective.

For example, entomologists, pathologists, or weed scientists could respond to a pesticide issue. However, the inclusion of the disciplines of economics, sociology, engineering, toxicology, and so on could strengthen such a response. The situation was often exacerbated by various groups who were not bound by the rigors of the scientific method. In such situations a more assertive voice made possible by a coalition of scientific societies and their representative disciplines would be more effective in countering such arguments.

In the final analysis, it is remarkable that such an organization could be formed. Indeed, it was brought about because some of the participants from the scientific societies were truly visionary leaders who also possessed many other important leadership skills. In addition, the process benefited from the fact that one of the early leaders and the first president, who also became the first executive vice president, was Charles Black, from Iowa State University. Black was a true scholar who possessed impeccable scientific credentials. His remarkable dedication and unwavering professionalism put CAST on a sound basis. Black's involvement was certainly an asset in demonstrating that those in the basic sciences could become involved in the larger picture of conveying information about agricultural science and technology to the news media, the public, and members of the US Congress, thus emphasizing the goal.

The early stages of any organization are the most critical, especially one that involved such a diverse population of participants. Black, by capitalizing on his sharp intellect and perseverance, provided the kind of inspired leadership necessary to hold such a diversified coalition intact. Furthermore, it did not hurt that he was soft spoken and not burdened with a superego. What he had was total dedication to scientific rigor and truth. Although not perfect, Black, perhaps more than any other person, held the coalition together sufficiently to enable the organization to become established.

Fortunately, in the very earliest days of CAST a number of distinguished agricultural scientists who held various leadership roles in agriculture also had influence in their respective scientific societies. Some of these early CAST visionaries included Cecil Howes, Bart Cardon, Fred Warren, Jack Carter, and Ed Crosby. These individuals came from widely different backgrounds, but all had one thing in common: they strongly supported the mission of CAST. Without their inspired leadership, CAST would not have gotten off the ground.

Another facet of the challenge is the differing role of leadership in some societies. For example, certain groups believe that the leadership functions primarily as management, and most real decisions are left to a vote of the membership. In other associations, the leadership can exercise a decision-making role. Clearly, it is challenging enough for a scientific society to exist and even more challenging for a consortium of such groups to develop. The challenge grows when trying to get a specific scientific society to truly appreciate how other disciplinary interests can help solve an issue that seemingly is a single discipline problem. By routinely employing a multidisciplinary approach to issues, an organization strengthens its response to most problems.

Financial Support for CAST

It was envisioned from the beginning that fiscal support would come from a variety of sources, including scientific societies, individual members, government grants and contracts, and industry. Some individuals and scientific groups believed that support from industry would exert undue influence on the quality of output by CAST. This occurred in spite of great care taken to isolate funding from the scientific efforts and actions of CAST to ensure that CAST's output did not inappropriately back the ideas of an industrial component. However, after lengthy debate and careful deliberation CAST was officially given life. Nevertheless, a number of the agriculture-related scientific societies chose not to be a part of the effort.

Although the major concern expressed by nonsupporters was the issue of funding, some controversial science and technology issues emerged as well, such as the use of antibiotics in livestock feed. As with all such issues, CAST dealt with this question by considering the best scientific information available at the time.

Restructuring and the Formation of the "New CAST"

Throughout their life span, most organizations experience both high and low points. Changes in situations often make it necessary to get out of the comfort zone and make bold changes just to survive. The challenges that existed when CAST was initiated have essentially remained and perhaps even grown in an ever-fluctuating economy. That CAST has survived and, indeed, been successful for forty years is a testimony to the perseverance of a few highly dedicated leaders, a few full-time staff members, and many part-time employees.

The success of CAST for four decades is evidence of the soundness of the original idea. Further strengthening CAST's success is the positive response by its target audiences, including the media, the US Congress, and the general public. In fact, CAST has received many accolades for its accomplishments. The new challenge was simply that the business model that had worked for forty years no longer provided sufficient support to sustain CAST. Consequently, its leaders had to act.

The eighth executive vice president, John Bonner, is a recent leader who recognized the new challenges (primarily financial) that CAST faced. Having both a science and a business background, he sensed something had to be done. Capitalizing on his business skills, he provided information to the board of directors, which rose to the occasion and made bold, necessary changes. As a result of the board's wisdom, a new CAST has recently taken shape, and it will need visionary leadership comparable to that required when CAST was initiated. The "new CAST" addresses some of the difficulties.

Figure 6. Popular publications and scientific information documents supplied by CAST.

The new structure provides for a small board of trustees whose members will be expected to pay all of their own personal expenses, a small board of directors whose members will receive travel reimbursement, and a larger board of representatives whose members will not receive travel support—a major change from previous practice. This restructuring will address several of the concerns, particularly lowering operation costs. Unfortunately, it will not alleviate the perceived conflict over the financial support that CAST derives from industry.

The Impact of CAST

CAST fulfills its mission through myriad activities such as publication projects and an array of sponsored activities (figure 6). From the outset, CAST was envisioned as a facilitator. In essence, it does not take positions on issues; rather, it facilitates the collaboration of appropriate scientists and other experts to address particular issues involving some aspect of agricultural science and technology. Consequently, CAST's output is the result of the efforts of agricultural task forces and panels empowered to address any given issue.

CAST's publications, which are highly regarded as a source of sound, science-based information written and reviewed by subject experts, include task-force reports, special publications, issue papers, and commentaries. One of the most popular recent publications is the CAST Issue Paper no. 45, "Agricultural Productivity Strategies for the Future—Addressing U.S. and Global Challenges."

This publication joins other very highly regarded efforts, particularly CAST Issue Paper no. 44, "Water, People, and the Future: Water Availability for Agriculture in the United States." A follow-on to the publication was the development of a video that summarizes the issue paper; that video has been exceedingly well received. One of CAST's recent publication efforts is a nine-part series: "Animal Agriculture's Future through Biotechnology." This example illustrates the importance of addressing certain issues from a multidisciplinary perspective. In addition to animal science, other areas that contribute to this issue are biotechnology, food safety, agricultural engineering, nutrition, immunology, animal welfare, and ethics.

A quick perusal of a list of CAST's efforts includes many timely, definitive, and important studies: "The Endangered Species Act: Interfacing with Agricultural and Natural Ecosystems"; "Food Safety and Fresh Produce: An Update"; "Carbon Sequestration, Greenhouse Gas Fluxes and Climate Change in U.S. Agriculture: Challenges and Opportunities for Mitigation"; and "Convergence of Agriculture and Energy: IV. Infrastructure Considerations for Biomass Harvest, Transportation, and Storage."

Over the years, CAST has conducted a multitude of activities to spread awareness of its mission, including a "National Food Day Dialogue," congressional breakfasts on the "Hill" in Washington, DC, and a publication for high school science teachers. CAST has organized and hosted special events on important topics such as agricultural biotechnology and the public; food safety, sufficiency, and security; and sustaining animal agriculture.

Other CAST activities include *Friday Notes,* a weekly e-newsletter providing links to current resource materials gleaned from more than 125 sources; symposia and conferences to promote communication among professionals in many disciplines of agricultural science; education and training workshops for hands-on learning; and international exchanges of scientific experts.

Recognizing the importance of educating young people about agriculture, CAST supports a wide array of student activities such as the Ag Day Essay Contest. CAST also arranges for individuals to provide briefings and offer scientific information to legislative and government personnel at local, state, and national levels.

With such a diverse portfolio of activities and an organizational composition that involves such a wide variety of scientific societies representing numerous professional and scientific disciplines, it is little wonder that maintaining an organization such as CAST is truly a highly desirable challenge.

A discussion of the founding and continuation of CAST would be incomplete without mentioning that Norman Borlaug was a charter member of CAST and author of the first CAST paper, "Agricultural Science and the Public." Borlaug has been recognized in many venues. He was the recipient of the Nobel Peace Prize, a Presidential Medal of Freedom, and the Congressional Gold Medal. The British publication *The Economist* credits Borlaug, who is often called the "father of the green revolution," with saving more lives than any other person who ever lived. He was a strong supporter of CAST until his death in September 2009. Clearly, he was an inspiring role model for many and contributed greatly to CAST's success.

Regrettably, there are also examples of situations in which stronger leadership and active involvement would have been of great benefit to CAST. For example, CAST is recognized as carrying out functions that are a part of the mission of the nation's colleges of agriculture, although from a much broader perspective. Consequently, one would think that administrative leaders of agriculture (department heads, deans, and vice presidents) at the nation's agricultural institutions would be among the strongest supporters of CAST. There are many excellent examples of these agricultural leaders actively supporting CAST. However, in view of the importance of communicating the science and technology of agriculture, a strong commitment by all agricultural administrative leaders is critical.

It is interesting to speculate about why some agricultural administrative leaders have not been active supporters of CAST. Although these individuals have considerable power and responsibility in their respective institutions, to support CAST would be using time, resources, and effort for the common good with little recognition of or credit for their respective institutions.

In defense of these leaders, however, they have exceedingly challenging jobs that place great demands on their time and resources. In their positions, they are accustomed to having individuals come to them when requesting support or action. Of course, CAST does not have the resources to take such individual approaches. Perhaps playing a small role is the fact that CAST had a truly grassroots beginning. There was no concerted effort to secure "buy-in" by administrative leaders. Furthermore, they allow their faculty to actively support CAST by participating in task forces and other CAST activities, which is no small contribution.

Another disappointment is that CAST has not been successful in developing a strong individual membership base. Even though there are very few arguments against the merit or efforts of CAST, far fewer than 1 percent of agricultural scientists in academia, government, and industry are members. Yet, on a positive note, almost all of the scientists who are invited to participate in a task force or on scientific panels quickly accept.

Although these aspects of leadership associated with CAST are disappointing, the visionary leadership that created the organization and is working on the "new CAST" reflects positively on the strength of the overall agricultural enterprise. The challenges in communicating information about the science and technology of agriculture can quite often be more effectively addressed by multiple disciplines from a wide array of scientific societies and institutions than by a single entity. However, bringing such diverse groups and interests together in order to reach consensus on issues requires great skill. That CAST has been quite successful in the past forty years is a testament to the validity of the scientific aspects of the model. The changing environment and the need for a better model to deal with the financial health of CAST require even stronger and more innovative leadership.

Leadership Perspective

The formation of CAST provides a physical manifestation of this work's definition of leadership as "the act and process of inspiring others to participate/collaborate in an endeavor oriented in a specific direction and/or intended to accomplish a particular goal or objective." It also validates the leadership model presented here, as it subscribes to its major and minor tenets. As an independent arbiter for important agricultural issues that require interdisciplinary and multidisciplinary treatments, along with the influence on a broad spectrum of its various programs, CAST is clearly an organization of immense value and potential. Its value was manifest in the essential cardinal virtues of Prudence, Justice, Temperance, and Fortitude, which spurred the formation of the organization. Examples include the initial impetus to form CAST (prudence and justice), the influence of the organization's publications and programs on important agricultural issues (temperance), and the commitment to continue important work on behalf of others in relative anonymity (fortitude). The "important" virtues were evident in the formation and early stages of CAST as well. Examples of thinking included the vision to recognize the need for such an organization, the willingness to function as agents of change, along with its inherent synergistic capabilities (creativity) and flexibility in its publications and programs. Acting included taking the initiative to form the organization, along with the confidence and resourcefulness it took to realize that ambition, the communication that occurred among the founders, and the ensuing communication that CAST motivated within the agricultural community and among its numerous constituents. Believing aspects included the trust and respect with which the project began, along with the optimism, tact, and enthusiasm that characterized the organization's founding and early years.

The requirement for a "new CAST," however, indicates that some or all of the essential elements were not maintained, thus requiring a substantial retooling of the institution in order for it to remain relevant and effective. In particular, CAST had lost its ability to satisfy the requirements of prudence and temperance, as it could no longer clearly justify its reason for existing, prioritize its responsibilities, recognize and accept the limitations of acceptable action, provide guidance for choosing among available alternatives, or reconcile the conflicts that arose among its various constituencies.

CAST failed to manifest success in several of the model's "important" virtues as well, including acting, thinking, and believing, which hindered its ability to garner appropriate levels of financial resources, support from the nation's agricultural institutions and/or "buy-in" by important administrative leaders, and a robust base of committed individual members, all of which diminished its ability to function as an agent of change for agriculture. Nevertheless, the core of the organization retained some essential aspects of thinking, including its sustained vision of its existence and ability to make an impact; acting, especially its communication role; and believing, particularly its ability to foster respect and trust while demonstrating tremendous humility, all of which was enough to sustain the organization and serve as a basis for the "new CAST."

Thus, the CAST case study provides broad validation for the work's leadership model in two ways: the formation and early years of CAST conform to the major and minor tenets of the model, and the diminishing effectiveness of CAST as an organization, which required the formation of a "new CAST," illustrates the inability of organizations to thrive without adhering to the essential elements of the model. In addition, the tendency of CAST to stray from the "important" elements of the model provides an example of "practical drift,"[3] which, if allowed to continue, leads to organizational failure. Providing dual examples of success and failure within a single organization, this case study is perhaps the most convincing example of the validity of the work's leadership model, as it demonstrates the model's applicability as a heuristic device and flexibility as an analytical tool.

Lessons Learned from Case Studies

We recognize that readers may have focused on different parts of this book, depending on their own experiences, interests, and background. Perhaps some will even have read most or all of the chapters. In this chapter we recapitulate some of the main points that caused us to decide that yet another book on leadership would be of use to those coming into or already in leadership roles in various parts of the food and agricultural system.

We hope readers will find the nontextbook approach refreshing and useful. The case studies present a variety of observations we have made during our careers, which have encompassed relatively diverse leadership roles. We have framed these studies as minibiographies that reflect our experiences and represent the most important characteristics of leadership in the context of a food and agricultural system. The general qualities of leadership that we deem the most critical in each case study are highlighted as part of the chapters on individual studies.

We share a common background in having been involved in military leadership for much of our professional lives. We have also been involved in substantial leadership roles in state and federal government, the private sector, and academia. One of us, a military historian by profession, brings academic rigor and contemporary knowledge of the literature on leadership to the book. All of us are both continuing students and practitioners of leadership in our common and separate career endeavors. Three of us were involved in initiating and sustaining formal leadership training programs for rising academic professionals who contemplated taking on academic leadership roles. This was initially the ESCOP leadership program, which grew to encompass all three agricultural parts of the land-grant system—research, extension, and resident education.

The book's preface discusses the purpose and focus of the book and describes what readers can expect. The first portion deals with the overarching qualities of leadership, which are the inherent point of departure for the more specific elements of individual and shared leadership illustrated here. The case studies illustrate the major elements of leadership, which are critical to developing and maintaining leadership in food and agricultural system careers. This chapter also brings the book to closure by summarizing some of the "take-home lessons" we believe are important.

Table 1 is a summary of the most important leadership qualities for each of the case studies. In fact, almost every case study would encompass all of leadership qualities in one form or another. The table highlights only the most salient qualities exhibited in each specific case study and is intended to be illustrative rather than inclusive regarding the major elements of leadership addressed. The columns show the case studies presented, and the rows contain the qualities of leadership that are presented and discussed in the chapter titled "Character: The Bedrock of Leaders and Leadership."

The chart emphasizes several important points collectively that each case study made individually:

> The essential attributes of wisdom, courage, moderation, and justice are in fact requisite for successful endeavors.

> Provided the four essential attributes were adhered to, the case studies indicate that success could have been attained with remarkable performance in anywhere from one to seventeen of the twenty "important" attributes, suggesting the indispensable influence of the essential attributes.

> The controlling ideas of each of the three components of the "important" attributes— acting, thinking, and believing—are of relatively equal value in terms of the overall outcomes described in the case studies.

	Facing Nature	Distributed Ag (AREC) Leader-ship	Closing / Relocating Programs	National Research Initiative	Battling Formosan Termites	Gather-ing of the Ag Clan	Seeing the Future	Leadership in State Ag Exp Stns	CAST
Prudence	Yes	Yes	Yes	Yes	Yes	Yes	Yes	Yes	Yes/No
Justice	Yes	Yes	Yes	Yes	Yes	Yes	Yes	Yes	Yes
emperance	Yes	Yes	Yes	Yes	Yes	Yes	Yes	Yes	Yes / No
Fortitude	Yes	Yes	Yes	Yes	Yes	Yes	Yes	Yes	Yes
Acting	Yes	Yes	Yes	Yes	Yes	Yes	Yes	Yes	Yes / No
Integrity		X	X					X	
Initiative	X	X	X	X	X			X	X
aking Risks			X						
mmunication	X	X	X	X	X	XX			XX
Confidence	X	X	X	X	X		X	X	X
Motivation	X	X		X	X		X		X
ssertiveness	X	X	X	X	X				
Bearing			X						
Thinking	Yes	Yes	Yes	Yes	Yes	Yes	Yes	Yes	Yes / No
Vision	X	X	X	X	X		X	X	XX
ecisiveness	X			X	X				
Flexibility	X	X	X	X	X				X
Creativity	X	X	X	X	X		X		X
bility to Be a hange Agent		X		X			X		X / 0
Believing	Yes	Yes	Yes	Yes	Yes	Yes	Yes	Yes	Yes / No
Trust	X	X	X	X	X			X	XX
Respect	X	X	X	X				X	XX
Optimism	X	X	X	X	X		X		X
Enthusiasm	X	X	X	X	X				X
Humility	X		X		X				X
Humor	X		X						
Tact	X		X	X	X				X

e chart emphasizes several important points made in each case study:

The essential attributes of Wisdom, Courage, Moderation, and Justice are vital to successful endeavors.

Provided the four essential attributes were adhered to, the case studies indicate that success could have been attained with anywhere from one to seventeen of the twenty "important" attributes, suggesting the indispensable influence of the essential attributes.

The controlling ideas of each of the three components of the "important" attributes (acting, thinking, and believing) are of relatively equal value in terms of the overall outcomes described in the case studies.

Within this group of case studies, the following attributes were particularly remarkable: initiative, communication, confidence, vision, creativity, trust, respect, and optimism.

Communication and vision were the most common of the "impact" attributes highlighted, followed closely by confidence and trust.

Within this group of case studies, the following attributes were particularly remarkable: initiative, communication, confidence, vision, creativity, trust, respect, and optimism.

In aggregate, communication and vision were the most prevalent of the "important" attributes highlighted, followed closely by confidence and trust. We hope that in reflecting on the messages in this book, readers will appreciate that the approach taken was intended to be descriptive and not prescriptive. We did not take a cookbook approach to leadership methods but presented a more philosophical description of the leadership principles. The case studies are drawn from a diverse set of specific illustrations of leadership principles that span the breadth of the food and agriculture system. Our intent was to place the overarching principles of leadership into a practical and explicit context in the form of experiences and outcomes that illustrate their application. The overarching messages that can be drawn from the case studies include the following main points—most of which point to the first two chapters of the book:

Leadership begins with an inherent or acquired set of guiding principles closely related to the personality and experience of individual leaders. In most cases, leaders are neither born nor made but reflect a combination of inherent traits and experiences. Most leaders are "people oriented" and apply the many qualities of leadership described in this book toward goals of the people they lead and the institutions they serve.

Applying the principles of good leadership to individual situations separates the managers from the leaders. This is the ability to apply the integrative process of bringing the pieces together, the combination of vision, planning, and execution that leads to (an old but useful truism) doing the right things and doing things right. As Gen. George S. Patton once said,

"A leader is one who can adapt principles to circumstances," suggesting the enduring value of certain principles and the art of leading well.

Leadership can be learned and evolves with experience; it involves both an experience-based intuition and a set of acquired skills that allow leaders to deal with the total picture—people, resources, politics, a vision of the future, and the current art of the possible.

Leadership involves both creating and responding to change. Creating change sometimes begins with a new vision or concept that is initially rejected by those affected and requires persistence to transition into practice. Sometimes new visions must await the evolution of the environment in which they are manifest to move to practice. Responding to change, either predicted or unexpected, is often highly situational. Leadership may emerge from and respond to new environments in which leaders find themselves. Several of the case studies illustrate how this occurs in practice. Effective leaders follow the maxim *carpe diem* [seize the day]. They get in front of the crowd and take advantage of being on the "steep part of the curve" of visionary rewards.

The case studies repeatedly show how leadership can be manifested by individuals or groups of people. Shared leadership is more challenging because it requires gaining the consensus of people with varying institutional and intellectual perspectives; strong-minded people with diverse perspectives, motivations, values, and desired outcomes. Leadership is manifested in different ways and often involves different kinds of leaders as new initiatives move from concept through advocacy and into practice. While shared leadership may be more challenging, it is obviously more rewarding in today's world of shared governance and interdisciplinary and interinstitutional engagements throughout the food and agriculture system.

We and the readers of this book probably share a common question or thought: How can the general principles illustrated in these case studies be applied to the challenges that will confront the next generation of leaders in food and agriculture? How will the basic principles and tenets of leadership in this field be manifested in an increasingly complex set of relationships—all operating in the context of the global village? The answers are likely to be specific to the situation or individual, but general principles will also apply. The following are illustrative but not inclusive of the environments in which future leaders will find themselves. The topics are by now familiar; applying the principles of leadership elaborated in this book will be exciting and rewarding:

Globalization of agriculture—production, trade, marketing

The international goal of achieving or at least improving food security for all people

Climate change and related environmental issues

Shrinking global base of natural resources—water, soil, and so on

Increasing regulatory constraints

Complex academic/private-sector/government relationships

The growing public and governmental concerns about food safety and the implications for the overall system of food and fiber production for national and international customers

The role of agriculture in achieving energy security for everyone as we end the era of fossil energy

The war against terrorism as it affects the biosecurity of the food and agriculture system

Increasing importance of faculty governance in academic institutions

A constantly evolving system of rewards for excellence in academic performance

Influence of the institutional and individual motivations to protect intellectual property rights and the Freedom of Information Act on planning, conducting, publishing, and applying research

Based on the ubiquity of agriculture and food production in the emerging global environment, we end where we began—by concluding with the hope that we have succeeded in creating a broad perspective on the main characteristics of leadership for use by those involved or interested in what may be the most important issue facing humankind in the twenty-first century.

Making Leadership Work for You

In its simplest definition, leadership is about motivating other people to follow you in a given direction to achieve a specific goal. The evolution of agriculture to an enterprise that is based more on science and technology rather than on resources requires a greater degree of visionary leadership. This trend is expected to project into the foreseeable future. We are witnessing a greater involvement of the social sciences and economics in agriculture, and the march of the planet toward greater globalization only exacerbates this trend. It emphasizes the critical position of leadership in the endeavor.

There was a time when a single scientist, perhaps with some understudy support, accomplished research alone and published papers with only the scientist's name as the author. The same can be said in the history of organizations and even government agencies when they first began. This is almost never seen today. *Team building* is the way we see effective agricultural programs carried out on the farm, in academia, and within industrial organizations and government programs. Team effort requires leadership regardless of whether the team is small or large. We have seen this in both our agricultural and military assignments. In addition to agricultural research leadership jobs, leadership principles for scientists show up in ancillary assignments, which may include leadership roles in other venues such as scientific societies, professional organizations, various associations, task forces, workgroups, strategic planning groups, and so on. Consequently, we are confident that the future success of agriculture is highly dependent upon the quality of leadership throughout the field. This can be achieved only by focusing education and training on strengthening and improving leadership skills. While it is important to begin developing leadership skills early in the educational process, it is equally important for existing personnel in agriculture to improve their leadership abilities, particularly as they accept greater responsibility.

If you ask who needs such training, we believe that almost every aspect of the agricultural enterprise benefits from leadership education and training. Newly appointed agricultural scientists are recruited and hired, usually after a thorough search process that involves an assessment of a candidate's academic education and training. Candidates who meet the demanding standards can be expected to have the potential for a successful career in science. However, one of the criteria often overlooked is an assessment of the candidate's leadership skills and ability. This is unfortunate because, in addition to science, a research scientist must provide leadership for technicians and staff, be involved in relevant scientific societies, and participate in a multitude of other aspects of a research program. Scientists must know how to sell their research idea when preparing a grant proposal. Even though individuals surviving the academic selection process are usually intelligent and highly motivated, they are often required to engage in on-the-job training to develop the leadership skills sufficient to lead their research enterprise. A similar scenario can be developed for those in industrial organizations and in government agencies. The situation becomes more critical with higher levels of responsibility. In fact, only those who have learned such skills usually succeed in the higher-level positions. An example of this can be found in almost any university; success as a faculty member is certainly no guarantee of success at a higher level of responsibility.

The first farmers and ranchers in the early days of our country were rugged individualists by necessity since they had to not only survive but also thrive while operating in near isolation. In contrast, modern farmers and ranchers must have a command of many of the technical aspects of farming and ranching to be successful. In addition, they must interface with a broad array of people and organizations that can affect the farm operations. Working effectively with such a myriad of groups requires an appreciation of leadership skills and ability. This is particularly important in working with commodity, trade, marketing, and a host of other organizations. For those whose careers take them into the world of government, either state or national, leadership skills become a critical tool for success. One of the reasons is that many programs in government require coordination between specific units and even departments and at the national level. Programs may even involve coordination with individuals in another cabinet agency.

This also is where the technical-production aspects of agriculture collide with politics. Almost all who are engaged in the agricultural enterprise must navigate various laws, regulations, and requirements to be successful. At higher levels of responsibility, we must learn to achieve the desired or necessary scientific goals at the policy level by being able to effectively compromise in the "art of the politically possible"—whether in the private sector, academia, or government. Even the individual scientist must comply with many rules, regulations, and policies while conducting research. The farmer must deal not only with production issues but also with labor issues, transportation, rules and regulations, farm programs, and a variety of laws concerning endangered species and environmental matters. Finding success in such situations requires effective leadership skills and ability. Finally, scientists either in industrial organizations or in governmental assignments have to constantly remember who is the "boss," whether it be a board of directors or a citizen of the state or even the nation, and leadership skills pay off at a high level in such an environment.

Indeed, from its beginnings, agriculture has always been and remains an inherently collective endeavor, making it among the most natural and authentic of leadership environments. To succeed, individuals must cooperate and collaborate, which requires them to interact and thus gives rise to requirements and opportunities for leadership. Accordingly, the agricultural community, while being a quintessentially natural activity, has also been one preternaturally disposed to individuals who are both practitioners and leaders. As social psychologists Constantine Sedikides and Marilynn B. Brewer posit, there are three levels of identity that one may develop—individual, relational, and collective—which are of increasing levels of complexity and effectiveness.[1] James Paul Gee tells us that, besides one's natural and institutional leadership identities, identities are created and constructed through discursive practices (i.e., physical actions and behaviors) and interactions within, between, and among affinity groups.[2] Thus, acting like a leader and interacting with others and groups within the agricultural community is essential to the development of one's identity as a leader. Recent advances in neuroscience bear this out. Farmers and ranchers have always had opportunities and reasons for interaction, but these occasions have likely been largely functional and pragmatic in nature and not necessarily oriented toward helping them develop their own leader identities in other than tangential and/or ancillary ways. This speaks to the explicit and deliberate need for leadership education and training within the agricultural community to foster, facilitate, and encourage such essential actions.

The case studies in this book illustrate a very small sample of the real-world aspects of leadership encountered in the agricultural sector. Additionally, in view of the vital role of leadership in the future of agriculture, we offer some observations and recommendations. The case studies serve only as examples of challenges that we or others have actually encountered, together with the approach that was utilized to reach a satisfactory solution.

Let us not forget that leaders in any agricultural enterprise will also likely be expected to deal with simple issues such as space utilization, nonproductive personnel, and priority in the use of special equipment. The leader will also have to deal with more serious issues such as sexual harassment, stealing, forgery, or misappropriation of funds. Similarly, the leader might encounter challenges such as staff members' utilizing improper purchasing procedures, as well as higher-authority individuals' appropriating resources assigned to your unit and staff or failing to follow regulations. These and many other problems require special leadership skills in order to arrive at a satisfactory solution.

We wish to share with you some observations and recommendations.

Observations

As agriculture becomes more sophisticated and complex, leadership skills become even more critical.

Agriculture is a highly diverse, constantly evolving enterprise, thereby requiring leadership skills in many areas.

The dynamic aspect of agriculture requires a constant utilization of new and different approaches.

Agricultural scientists and administrators usually begin their assignment with little formal education and training in leadership.

Agricultural scientists and administrators often improve over time, lending credence to the success of on-the-job training. Some agricultural scientists and administrators never improve.

A successful outcome in the future of agriculture requires major improvements in leadership skills throughout the field.

There is a need for improvement of leadership skills throughout academia, government, and industry. Also important are commodity and trade organizations and all professional groups associated with agriculture.

Quality leadership can improve almost any situation and can often prevent disasters.

Recommendations

Some type of leadership education/training should be a part of the academic curriculum for all agriculture students.

Those who are appointed to various positions in agriculture should participate in some type of leadership training as a condition of employment. Consider these examples:

Academic Faculty and Staff: Colleges of agriculture should develop a leadership program for new hires (faculty and staff).

Deans, Directors, and Department Heads in Academia: Within one year of their appointment, these individuals should participate in a "system" leadership-development program or comparable leadership training and development program.

Commodity and Trade: Encourage those individuals appointed to responsible positions in commodity or trade groups to participate in a state leadership or comparable program. If the state does not have a program, then start one. Most states already have one, although they are often poorly funded.

Farmers and Ranchers: Leadership development among farmers and ranchers is mostly an ad hoc process with little direction or coordination. Agricultural leaders in each state should make a concerted effort to develop some type of leadership-development effort for agriculturally related individuals not included in some of the foregoing groups.

Agricultural Industry Personnel: For new hires in industry, there should be some effort to provide a form of leadership training or leadership experience, which will involve joining another organization's leadership-development program.

Government Employees: Individuals who accept an appointment for government service should commit to some form of leadership skill enhancement. Such opportunities can be found in government-supported courses and can also include some of the state-sponsored leadership development programs and even computer-based courses offered online.

If you are in a position of authority, ensure that your subordinates receive appropriate leadership education, training, and experience.

Emerging leaders in each of the preceding categories should become students of leadership, developing their capacity to improve their organizations and provide guidance to subordinates in developing their own leadership skills.

All individuals should assess their leadership strengths and weaknesses and identify ways in which they can strengthen and hone their personal leadership skills.

All new hires in academia would do well to have a mentor to assist them to become as effective as possible. The mentor should encourage each new hire and offer suggestions and counsel to improve the individual's leadership skills.

Individuals should develop a leadership-development plan for personal improvement. Such a plan should include a development program, benchmarks, accomplishments, and both short-term and long-term goals for improvement. Personal progress should be reported to the mentors.

When appointed to a position of leadership, individuals should seriously review all available information about the position. Avoid reinventing the wheel. Build on what others have already discovered.

Individuals should at all times be cognizant that they are on display and set a proper and appropriate leadership example for others.

Academic institutions engaged in agriculture should include leadership training and skills development for their students. Such programs should be made available to individuals engaged in every aspect of the agricultural enterprise.

In the final analysis, leadership is all about getting the right things accomplished in the right way at the right time. Anyone engaged in any aspect of agriculture should strive to achieve this goal. Developing and improving leadership skills and ability are definite moves in the right direction to make this happen.

Agriculture is no different from most other of life's endeavors. Leadership is important for success. Consequently, "making leadership work for you" is a key to that success.

Appendixes

HOW DOES THE SCIENTIFIC AGRICULTURAL SYSTEM WORK?

Leadership and its mechanisms can often be influenced by both the structures and the program-approval process that organizations use. These appendixes present three examples of such processes as frequently used in the United States.

Structure often drives *program,* and *program* can oftentimes influence *structure.* Thus, these appendices will help the reader who wishes to understand how various parts of the system work. *Program approval* is the door-opener for successful projects, so each appendix summarizes structure and ways in which projects are funded.

Appendix A

The Land-Grant System: A Key to America's Dream?
How Does It Function?

The Morrill Act, passed by the US Congress in 1862, provided for the land-grant colleges and was a great stimulus to the development of this country. That bill directed these colleges to focus on two fundamental areas of building an economy: agriculture and the "mechanic arts" (engineering and manufacturing) while not excluding other aspects of higher learning.

The importance of the Morrill Act is often overlooked. It is among the most important legislation ever passed by any governing body. Signed into law by President Lincoln at the height of the American

Civil War, it held that higher learning was not necessarily for the affluent; rather, access to higher learning was for all and focused on topics that could build an economy and therefore a nation.

As many states began teaching programs in agriculture, it soon became evident that available scientific-based agricultural subject matter was lacking. This simple fact became more and more obvious. Many states embarked on scientific investigations to fill some of the information voids. While such efforts are highly commendable, it soon became evident that the real need was for a more comprehensive and unified system: enter Congressman William Henry Hatch of Missouri. The legislation that bears his name, the Hatch Act of 1887, provided for an agricultural experiment station in each state.[1] Among other things, the forward-looking legislation provided for a loosely unified system of federal funding joined with state funding. This flexible mechanism would enable each state experiment station director to address special local needs. Funding for agricultural research in the following years was designed to foster and enhance collaboration among stations and states. Formula funds provided each state experiment station with base support, and the results were shared with other state experiment stations. The regional research funding (RRF) mechanism supported a classic means of encouraging collaboration. In recent years competitive grant funding has been added to the agricultural research agenda, which in many cases has allowed greater flexibility since formula funds provide the strong needed base and competitive grants allow for an expanded scientific perspective. Grant funds provide substantial funding to enhance research in a specific area that tends to be nation- or regionwide.

The next logical step in fulfilling the vision of supporting agriculture was to get the information and technology, which were developed through research, to the farmers. Thus was born the concept of extension. Senator Hoke Smith of Georgia and Rep. A. F. Lever of South Carolina were responsible for the legislation—often referred to as the Smith-Lever Act of 1914—that created the Cooperative Extension Service (CES).

The Smith-Lever legislation did more than provide for a delivery system for agricultural information and technology. It also made all agricultural programs relevant and encouraged collaboration among all parties to make them successful.

To address research needs in forestry, Congressman Clifford McIntire of Maine and Sen. John Stennis of Mississippi developed legislation (McIntire-Stennis Act of 1962) that provided support for such research in each state.

Two groups were not specifically provided for in the 1862 Morrill legislation: African Americans and Native Americans. Toward the end of the nineteenth century it was recognized that these groups have much to offer, and Congress initiated a remedy. Consequently, legislation was enacted in 1890 (often called the Second Morrill Act) that created land-grant colleges and universities directed at the African American population. Legislation enacted in 1994 provided for land-grant college support for Native Americans. These later two bills ensured that the spirit of the original 1862 Morrill Act now worked for all Americans.

There is a common theme here: the vital need for collaboration among all who are involved in the various programs. Everyone needs to contribute quality time, which will ensure the strength and viability of the system.

The active participation of agricultural leaders from the many states helps to accomplish the mission. First, by working together, specific problems can be identified before they become major problems. Then, by such collaboration, greater effort can be focused on a given challenge.

The tripartite mission (teaching, research, and extension) of the land-grant university system has proven to be a highly successful model for the support of agriculture.

FUNDING OF PROJECTS

Funding for the state agricultural experiment station (SAES) program involves USDA support in the formula funds based on several criteria in each state, plus funds provided by each state's legislature. Additionally, the US Congress provides special grants for specific projects. In terms of project approval in the land-grant system, formula funds are approved by the director and periodically reviewed by the National Institute of Food and Agriculture (NIFA) using the mechanism developed by its predecessor, the Cooperative State Research, Education, and Extension Services (CSREES). Generally they also undergo review at the state level, often including input from related industries (e.g., wheat or corn producers). Included is a scheduled, periodic site review of each project that receives such federal funding and involves scientists from other organizations such as SAES and ARS or from industry. Some of the scientists are very experienced in the competitive-grants approach and do well in the National Research Initiative (which in 2009 became the USDA Agricultural and Food Research Initiative [AFRI] as part of NIFA, which was authorized in the 2007 Farm Bill). These researchers also frequently compete for grants from the National Science Foundation, National Institutes of Health, and other federal programs, as well as from private foundations. The key of the competitive-grants program is to ensure the quality of projects. The questions addressed specifically include the following:

What problems are to be researched?
Why are they important?
What is the research hypothesis?
How will the hypothesis be tested?
Is the right group of scientists involved?

The State Cooperative Extension System receives formula funds from NIFA, as well as from the state legislatures and counties (parishes).

Thus, the CES system is a tripartite-funded program and, like the SAES, is based on decisions made by the state director, which are backed up by reviews, including those from the USDA-NIFA.

The vigor of within-state reviews is influenced by priority needs, available talent, and the decisions of the state legislature, in addition to those of the director of the State Agriculture Research System, the Cooperative Extension System, or the academic program in agriculturally related disciplines.[2] The standards are high, for the periodic review by scientists from other states challenge the very integrity of each project.

Further, in numerous instances an SAES or a CES project also has external funding from a granting agency or foundation. Finally, the success of the state-level agriculture research, teaching, and extension has proved its extraordinary impact throughout the more than one hundred years of its existence.

Appendix B

The USDA's Agricultural Research Service: Focus on National and International Issues

The Agricultural Research Service (ARS) is the USDA's in-house research organization for national and international issues. It provides research support for other USDA operating units such as the Food Safety and Inspection Service and the Animal and Plant Health Inspection Service. With about eight thousand scientists and staff conducting one thousand projects, it is the world's largest agricultural research organization. With its headquarters in Washington, DC, its roughly one hundred operational laboratories are divided into eight geographical areas supporting the nation and its territories. Many of the laboratories are actually on land-grant campuses, but regional research laboratories are self-contained, as is the very large USDA-ARS-Beltsville Agricultural Research Center, which is in Maryland.

Major regional research centers are located in each of the four agricultural areas of the country (New Orleans, Louisiana; Wyndmore, Pennsylvania; Peoria, Illinois, and Albany, California.) The administrator, key staff members, and the area directors meet regularly to develop and implement program plans.

The ARS has been a critical part of the USDA for many years, dating back to early seed testing, but the agency was codified under its current title in 1956.

FUNDING OF PROJECTS

The US Congress requires all projects within the ARS to undergo a thorough review by scientific talent beyond the ARS itself. This has evolved into as rigorous a review as is seen in any scientific granting or funding organization. It is based on an Office of Scientific Quality Review (OSQR) and uses a series of scientific panels specific to major areas of research. The scientific quality review officer is selected generally for a two-year appointment and is one of the top research leaders in the agency.

The panels are based on talent. At last count, 76 percent of the panel members came from academia, 13 percent from industry, 8 percent from government agencies, and 2 percent from other sources, while up to 1 percent were former ARS scientists.

The approach is very much like that required by the National Science Foundation (NSF) or the National Institutes of Health (NIH) for competitive grants. Although the OSQR does not award a certain amount of money to each funded proposal, *no project can use ARS funding until it is approved by the OSQR panel and the scientific quality review officer.* The award is made through the administrator's staff and the area directors but only after the successful OSQR approval process.

How does the system work? It begins with the drafting of a project proposal by an ARS scientist who will serve as the leader of the proposed project. The proposal typically undergoes an internal review within ARS on its way to OSQR. The assessment includes external, scientific, prospective, peer, and competitive reviews—a real dialogue between OSQR and ARS scientists. The ARS National Program Staff has input on every project reviewed. The key is to tell the "story" of the research and why it is needed to do so in an integrated and scientific format with a clear argument regarding how the results can be "marketed." The criteria include (a) the adequacy of the approach and the research procedures, (b) the probability of successfully accomplishing the project's objectives, and (c) the scientific merit and significance of the proposed research. The OSQR process entails several categories of action class scores, namely (a) no revision, (b) minor revision, and (c) moderate revision, all of which reflect a generally feasible project that can ultimately be approved by the scientific quality review officer. Two more categories include (d) major revision and (e) not feasible; with these, the project will be approved only after a re-review by the panel, which may take place after the lead scientist overhauls the proposal. Some projects are not approved, and a different project is necessary. Annual checks and balances are a part of the ongoing process.

OTHER USDA AGENCIES

In addition to the ARS, the USDA has other research-driven agencies such as the Economic Research Service and the US Forest Service. For specifics on each of these, the reader is referred to the information office of these agencies.

Appendix C

The Industrial Approach to Research: Diverse Foci Linked to Industrial Economic Effects

The variations in industrial approaches to research are so great that it is not possible to show one best approach or, for that matter, even the structure. However, let's look at an example that shows the principles that industrial organizations make use of. Remember that the key driving force in industry, indeed in agricultural industries, is *profit!* So perhaps we can look at a type of structure and then address ways to fund this research. Corporate structures often involve specific department heads such as president or CEO and departments such as operations, sales and marketing, finance, corporate services, or research and development.

The entire organization responds to a corporate strategic plan, in which all departments participate. The initial step is usually to determine the foundation and, therefore, the guidelines of the plan. These often include the management principals, common goals, efforts to strengthen communications among departments, teamwork atmosphere, ways to involve employees in the actions, and the criteria for measuring results, always leading to *profits.* Often the action plan involves *management by objectives,* recognizing both strengths and weaknesses in the organization and plan. It also likely involves an implementation schedule.

The imprimatur for almost any corporate long-range plan comes from the board (board of directors in many cases), which provides both input and approval. The next step involves the administration and control of the plans, which is usually associated with periodic meetings to review the results to date.

FUNDING FOR RESEARCH AND DEVELOPMENT

Generally the leader of the R and D arm of the organization presents a detailed request for investment dollars. The request will specify (a) why it is important (goal/mission), (b) what it will cost, (c) what the needs are for people, especially scientists in the program, (d) approximately how long it will be before results can be seen, (e) what the likely results will be in terms of forging ahead of competitors and in terms of profit, and (f) what the apparent balance is between investment and benefits. Finally, the question is asked, what does the project do for the organization's image?

More specifically, when considering whether to explore a project, the company will often ask the following types of questions:

1. Is there a tangible and/or an unsatisfied need that the concept can solve?
2. How long will the project take from discovery to launch, and what resources will be required?
3. What is the value of the product/technology (e.g., number of acres, types of crops)?
4. Where will this product bring farmers' value?
5. Are intellectual property policies in place to provide a reasonable return on investment to justify the project?
6. Do farmers, the ag industry, and the downstream food chain support the need for this new product?
7. Do we have the tools and talent required to prove the proof of concept?
8. What regulatory hurdles might need to be managed along the way?

Research and development may include improving current products or launching a brand-new product. It may also involve building on some other organization's success (piggybacking) or require the organization's scientists to seek dollars from a limited source of funding within the company, in essence competing with other departments of the organization.

Frequently, industry will wish to develop partnerships with other companies and establish scientific cooperation with university faculty and federal laboratories. Specific laws outline how to do this with federal laboratories.

Notes

Leadership in the Agricultural Environment

1. Hamilton, "Agriculture's Sustainable Future."
2. Eldredge and Gould, "Punctuated Equilibria."
3. *History of American Agriculture.*
4. Tweeten and Thompson, "Long-Term Global."
5. Burns, *Leadership,* 2.
6. Bass, *Stodgill's Handbook,* 5.
7. W. K. Kellogg Foundation, Policy Advocacy Comments, October 1, 2007.

Character: The Bedrock of Leaders and Leadership

1. Toner, *Morals under the Gun,* 59.
2. Ibid., 61.
3. Ibid., 74.
4. Ibid., 87.
5. Ibid., 133–34.
6. Ibid., 110.
7. Little, Wilson, and Moore, *Applied Logic.*

Case Studies

1. Covey, *8th Habit.*
2. The committee felt strongly that if a leadership program was going to be successful, it had to be endorsed and supported by the experiment station directors. Consequently, they should be willing to pay for it. This turned out to be true.
3. Snook, *Friendly Fire,* 24, 186.

Making Leadership Work for You

1. Sedikides and Brewer, eds., *Individual Self,* 1–2. This concept is developed further by Day and Harrison, "Multilevel, Identity-Based Approach."
2. Gee, "Identity as an Analytic Lens."

Appendixes

1.   State Agricultural Experiment Station (SAES). New York and Connecticut each established two separate stations.
2.   Modest USDA funding has been available for academic programs to ensure that the next generation of agriculturalists is well educated.

Bibliography

Army Leadership. 1999. US Army FM 22–100. Washington, DC: Headquarters, US Army.

Bass, Bernard N. 1990. *Stodgill's Handbook of Leadership.* New York: Free Press.

Bennis, Warren. 1989. *On Becoming a Leader.* New York: Basic Books/Perseus Books Group.

Burns, James MacGregor. 1978. *Leadership.* New York: Harper and Row.

———. 2003. *Transforming Leadership: A New Pursuit of Happiness.* New York: Grove.

Collins, Jim. 2001. *Good to Great: Why Some Companies Make the Leap . . . and Others Don't.* New York: Harper Collins.

Covey, Stephen R. 1992. *Principle-Centered Leadership.* New York: Fireside.

———. 1989. *The Seven Habits of Highly Effective People.* New York: Free Press.

———. 2004. *The 8th Habit: From Effectiveness to Greatness.* New York: Free Press.

Day, David V., and Michelle M. Harrison. 2007 "A Multilevel, Identity-Based Approach to Leadership Development." *Human Resource Management Review* 17: 365–67.

Eldredge, Niles, and S. J. Gould. 1972. "Punctuated Equilibria: A Gradualism." In *Models in Paleobiology,* ed. T. J. M. Schopf, 82–115. San Francisco: Freeman, Cooper.

Enriquez, Juan. 2001. *As the Future Catches You: How Genomics & Other Forces Are Changing Your Life, Work, Health & Wealth.* New York: Crown.

Gardner, Howard W. 1995. *Leading Minds: An Anatomy of Leadership.* New York: Basic Books/Perseus Books Group.

Gardner, John W. 1990. *On Leadership.* New York: Free Press.

Gee, James Paul. 2009. "Identity as an Analytic Lens for Research in Education." June 17. Pages 3–16, http://www.jamespaulgee.com/node/18.

Goffee, Rob, and Gareth Jones. 2006. *Why Should Anyone Be Led by You? What It Takes to Be an Authentic Leader.* Boston: Harvard Business School Press.

Gostick, Adrian, and Chester Elton. 2009. *The Carrot Principle: How the Best Managers Use Recognition to Engage Their People, Retain Talent, and Accelerate Performance.* New York: Free Press.

Greenleaf, Robert K. 1977. *Servant Leadership: A Journey into the Nature of Legitimate Power and Greatness.* New York: Paulist Press.

Hamilton, Richard. 2009. "Agriculture's Sustainable Future: Breeding Better
Crops." *Scientific American* (June). http://www.scientificamerican.com/article.
cfm?id=agricultures-sustainable-future.

Heifetz, Ronald A. 1994. *Leadership without Easy Answers*. Cambridge, Mass.:
Belknap Press of Harvard University Press.

Hesselbein, Francis, and Eric K. Shinseki. 2004. *Be, Know, Do: Leadership the Army
Way: Adapted from the Official Army Leadership Manual*. San Francisco: Jossey-
Bass.

History of American Agriculture, 1607–2002, A. 2000. ERS-Post-12. Washington,
DC: Economic Research Services. Http://www.agclassroom.org/gan/timeline/.

Huseman, Richard C., and John D. Hatfield. 1989. *Managing the Equity Factor . . .
or "After All I've Done for You."* Boston: Houghton Mifflin.

Johnson, Spencer. 1998. *Who Moved My Cheese? An Amazing Way to Deal with
Change in Your Work and in Your Life*. New York: Putnam.

Kellerman, Barbara. 2004. *Bad Leadership: What It Is, How It Happens, Why It Happens*. Boston: Harvard Business School Press.

Kerr, Norwood A. 1987. *The Legacy . . . a Centennial History of the State Agricultural Experiment Stations*. Columbia: Missouri Agricultural Experiment Station,
University of Missouri–Columbia.

Kotter, John P. 1996. *Leading Change*. Boston: Harvard Business School Press.

Kouzes, James M., and Barry Z. Posner. 2002. *The Leadership Challenge*, 3rd ed. San
Francisco: Jossey-Bass.

Leadership Statements and Quotes. 1985. Department of the Army, Pamphlet
600–65. Washington, DC: Department of the Army.

Little, Winston Woodard, W. Harold Wilson, and W. Edgar Moore. 1955. *Applied
Logic*. Boston: Houghton Mifflin.

Miller, Zell. 1996. *Corps Values: Everything You Need to Know I Learned in the
Marines*. Marietta, Ga.: Longstreet.

Northouse, Peter G. 1997. *Leadership: Theory and Practice*. Thousand Oaks, Calif.:
Sage.

Peddiwell, J. Abner. 2004. *The Saber-Tooth Curriculum*. New York: McGraw-Hill.

Peters, Thomas J., and Robert H. Waterman. 1982. *In Search of Excellence*. New
York: HarperCollins.

Safire, William, and Leonard Safir, eds. 1991. *Leadership*. New York: Fireside.

Sedikides, Constantine, and Marilyn B. Brewer, eds. 2001. *Individual Self, Relational
Self, Collective Self*. Philadelphia: Psychology Press.

Snook, Scott. 2002. *Friendly Fire: The Accidental Shootdown of U.S. Black Hawks
over Northern Iraq*. Princeton, N.J.: Princeton University Press).

Toner, James H. 2005. *Morals under the Gun: The Cardinal Virtues, Military*

Ethics, and American Society. Paperback edition. Lexington: University Press of Kentucky.

Tweeten, Luther, and Stanley R. Thompson. 2008. "Long-Term Global Agricultural Output Supply-Demand Balance and Real Farm and Food Prices." Department of Agricultural, Environmental, and Development Economics. Working Paper, AEDE-WP 0044–08. Ohio State University, Columbus, Ohio.

Tzu, Sun. 1963. *The Art of War.* Trans. Samuel B. Griffith. Oxford: Oxford University Press.

Williamson, Porter B. 1988. *Gen. Patton's Principles for Life and Leadership.* Tucson: Management and Systems Consultants.

About the Authors

JOHN PATRICK JORDAN has taught chemistry and biochemistry as well as conducting research in space medicine. He completed the Harvard Institute for Educational Management program, was director of the university-wide Biology Core Program at Colorado State University, became university-wide official responsible for the Experiment Station, and later oversaw the Cooperative Extension Service. For over eleven years, he was the administrator (CEO) of the USDA's Cooperative State Research Service and later, the director of the Agricultural Research Service's Southern Regional Research Center. He also served for twenty-five years as Encyclopaedia Britannica's *Yearbook of Science and the Future* author for agriculture. His PhD is from The University of California, Davis.

GALE A. BUCHANAN served as a professor and director of the Alabama Agricultural Experiment Station and then as dean and director of the University of Georgia, College of Agricultural and Environmental Sciences. His last administrative assignment was as USDA chief scientist and undersecretary for research, education and economics. Other leadership roles include serving as chair of the Board on Agriculture Assembly of the National Association of State Universities and Land Grant Colleges and as president and chair of the board of trustees of the Council for Agricultural Science and Technology. Iowa State University conferred his PhD.

NEVILLE P. CLARKE conducted research in aerospace physiology in support of the US manned spaceflight program, directed aerospace medicine research across the United States Air Force, was associate dean of the college of veterinary medicine and director of the Texas Agricultural Experiment Station at Texas A&M, executive director of the Southern Association of Agricultural Experiment Station Directors, and director of the Department of Homeland Security National Center for Foreign Animal Disease Defense. He currently serves as special assistant to the vice chancellor of agriculture at Texas A&M for program development. He earned a DVM from Texas A&M University and a PhD from the School of Medicine at the University of Washington.

KELLY C. JORDAN, a retired United States Army officer, is a military historian and leadership scholar. Earning a BA from the Virginia Military Institute and an MA and PhD from The Ohio State University, he served for over twenty-one years on active duty and on the faculties of six educational institutions, including the US Military Academy, US Naval War College, and the University of Notre Dame. The author of numerous publications, his most recent scholarship is in the areas of leadership studies and adolescent leader and character development. He is currently the Commandant of Cadets at Culver Military Academy.

Index

Page numbers followed by *italic* abbreviations refer to photos (*ph*) and figures (*fig*).